I0417185

PROGRESS AND CHALLENGES IN THE WESTERN BALKANS

HEARING

BEFORE THE

SUBCOMMITTEE ON EUROPE, EURASIA, AND EMERGING THREATS

OF THE

COMMITTEE ON FOREIGN AFFAIRS HOUSE OF REPRESENTATIVES

ONE HUNDRED FOURTEENTH CONGRESS

FIRST SESSION

APRIL 29, 2015

Serial No. 114–30

Printed for the use of the Committee on Foreign Affairs

Available via the World Wide Web: http://www.foreignaffairs.house.gov/ or
http://www.gpo.gov/fdsys/

U.S. GOVERNMENT PUBLISHING OFFICE

94–387PDF   WASHINGTON : 2015

For sale by the Superintendent of Documents, U.S. Government Publishing Office
Internet: bookstore.gpo.gov   Phone: toll free (866) 512–1800; DC area (202) 512–1800
Fax: (202) 512–2104   Mail: Stop IDCC, Washington, DC 20402–0001

COMMITTEE ON FOREIGN AFFAIRS

EDWARD R. ROYCE, California, *Chairman*

CHRISTOPHER H. SMITH, New Jersey
ILEANA ROS-LEHTINEN, Florida
DANA ROHRABACHER, California
STEVE CHABOT, Ohio
JOE WILSON, South Carolina
MICHAEL T. McCAUL, Texas
TED POE, Texas
MATT SALMON, Arizona
DARRELL E. ISSA, California
TOM MARINO, Pennsylvania
JEFF DUNCAN, South Carolina
MO BROOKS, Alabama
PAUL COOK, California
RANDY K. WEBER SR., Texas
SCOTT PERRY, Pennsylvania
RON DeSANTIS, Florida
MARK MEADOWS, North Carolina
TED S. YOHO, Florida
CURT CLAWSON, Florida
SCOTT DesJARLAIS, Tennessee
REID J. RIBBLE, Wisconsin
DAVID A. TROTT, Michigan
LEE M. ZELDIN, New York
TOM EMMER, Minnesota

ELIOT L. ENGEL, New York
BRAD SHERMAN, California
GREGORY W. MEEKS, New York
ALBIO SIRES, New Jersey
GERALD E. CONNOLLY, Virginia
THEODORE E. DEUTCH, Florida
BRIAN HIGGINS, New York
KAREN BASS, California
WILLIAM KEATING, Massachusetts
DAVID CICILLINE, Rhode Island
ALAN GRAYSON, Florida
AMI BERA, California
ALAN S. LOWENTHAL, California
GRACE MENG, New York
LOIS FRANKEL, Florida
TULSI GABBARD, Hawaii
JOAQUIN CASTRO, Texas
ROBIN L. KELLY, Illinois
BRENDAN F. BOYLE, Pennsylvania

AMY PORTER, *Chief of Staff*   THOMAS SHEEHY, *Staff Director*
JASON STEINBAUM, *Democratic Staff Director*

———————

SUBCOMMITTEE ON EUROPE, EURASIA, AND EMERGING THREATS

DANA ROHRABACHER, California, *Chairman*

TED POE, Texas
TOM MARINO, Pennsylvania
MO BROOKS, Alabama
PAUL COOK, California
RANDY K. WEBER SR., Texas
REID J. RIBBLE, Wisconsin
DAVID A. TROTT, Michigan

GREGORY W. MEEKS, New York
ALBIO SIRES, New Jersey
THEODORE E. DEUTCH, Florida
WILLIAM KEATING, Massachusetts
LOIS FRANKEL, Florida
TULSI GABBARD, Hawaii

CONTENTS

_____

PROGRESS AND CHALLENGES IN THE WESTERN BALKANS

WEDNESDAY, APRIL 29, 2015

HOUSE OF REPRESENTATIVES,
SUBCOMMITTEE ON EUROPE, EURASIA, AND EMERGING THREATS,
COMMITTEE ON FOREIGN AFFAIRS,
Washington, DC.

The subcommittee met, pursuant to notice, at 2 o'clock p.m., in room 2200 Rayburn House Office Building, Hon. Dana Rohrabacher (chairman of the subcommittee) presiding.

Mr. ROHRABACHER. I call to order this hearing of the Subcommittee on Europe, Eurasia, and Emerging Threats. Today's topic is progress and challenges in the Western Balkans.

After the ranking member and I each take 5 minutes to make opening remarks, each other member, if they so choose, will have the opportunity for making an opening statement as well. We will then proceed with our first panel of witnesses and without objection, all members will have 5 days to submit their statements or questions or extraneous material for the record. Hearing no objection, so ordered.

It has been almost exactly 2 years since the last time the subcommittee held a hearing on this region. I am pleased to again be returning to this important topic and to be able to hear from such informed witnesses. We all know the tragic history of the breakup of Yugoslavia during the 1990s. Yet, it is remarkable that today, every country in the region, including Serbia, is in some way seeking greater integration with European institutions. I congratulate Croatia, for example, which is perhaps the foremost example of this on their successful accession into the European Union in 2013. And while the region has witnessed some major steps forward over the last two decades including the independence of Kosovo, the pace of progress appears to have slowed and perhaps even regressed in certain cases.

Later this year, we will celebrate the 20-year anniversary of the Dayton Peace Accords which ended the Bosnian War. Reaching that agreement was an admirable diplomatic accomplishment. Yet, the political framework that ended the fighting has proven structurally unable to build a state which governs effectively or meets the expectations of its people.

I noted that over the weekend, the leader of the Republic of Srpska called for a referendum to determine if the Serb enclave in Bosnia should break away unless it is granted further autonomy. Clearly, the current arrangement in Bosnia is not working. In Macedonia, the exposure of a massive internal surveillance scheme has rocked that small nation, highlighting the immense challenges of building a state which respects the rule of law and the rule of law both inside the government and the rule of law outside the government.

Next door, EU brokered peace talks between Serbia and Kosovo just a few years ago, resulting in an agreement entitled ''Principles of Governing the Normalization of Relations.'' While we are all happy that a solution was reached between these two sides, there remains ample reason for concern. I remain doubtful about the prospect of integrating Serbs, for example, who live in the northern part of Kosovo and I am somewhat doubtful about them integrating into the rest of the country. If the Serb community in the northern part of Kosovo which is to be governed by Belgrade, we should acknowledge their right to determine for themselves what country they will live in and make their own self-determination. This is the same principle, I might add, that led us to support the Albanian Kosovars in their desire for self-determination two decades ago.

In closing, the Western Balkans collectively have been aided by deployment of at least three separate NATO missions which included a significant contingent of U.S. military personnel who I visited over the years. Billions of dollars have been spent by the European Union and our own Government to support economic development, reduce ethnic tensions, and build modern states. Between 1990 and 2012, USAID spent over $1.7 billion aid dollars to help the Western Balkans. And what has that huge sum of money accomplished over the years? What about the diplomatic accomplishments, what have they achieved or what are their efforts anyway? And has outside engagement reached an effective limit there in that part of the world? And to get answers for some of those questions and others, we will hear from our witnesses today.

Panel 1, first of all—Mr. Sires, would you like to have an opening statement? And then I will introduce the witnesses.

Mr. SIRES. Thank you, Mr. Chairman, for holding this hearing today to evaluate the state of the affairs in the Balkans. Since the mid-1990s, the region has undergone a great transformation as the wars have ended and political and economic reforms have set in. The region also progressed toward greater integration with European and transatlantic institutions. While great improvements have been made in the Balkans, various challenges still remain including dealing with the impact of Kosovo's independence and the on-going fight against organized crime and corruption in the region.

As we have witnessed over the past year, Russia continues to get influence outside of the borders, forcing the surrounding regions, including the Balkans to be on high alert. More than ever, it is imperative that we continue to be engaged in the Balkans to ensure democracy, security, and prosperity in the region. And I look forward to hearing from the esteemed panels that we have today. Thank you.

Mr. ROHRABACHER. All right, we will proceed. And when Congressman Meeks arrives, he will be free to have his opening statement as well.

Our witnesses for Panel 1 are Deputy Assistant Secretary Hoyt Yee who is appointed to his current position in the Bureau of European and Eurasian Affairs in September 2013. He is a career foreign service officer and previously stationed in Montenegro, in Greece, and most recently, as the DCM in Croatia. So he obviously knows the region.

Susan Fritz is the Acting Assistant Administrator for USAID in Europe and Eurasia Bureau. She is a 25-year veteran of USAID and has significant experience in the region as well. She served as the Mission Director in Serbia and the Deputy Mission Director for Kosovo. So with that said, I will introduce the second panel when you are done. If you could proceed with 5 minute opening statements. The rest of your statement will be made part of the record and then we will proceed.

Mr. Yee.

STATEMENT OF MR. HOYT BRIAN YEE, DEPUTY ASSISTANT SECRETARY, BUREAU OF EUROPEAN AND EURASIAN AFFAIRS, U.S. DEPARTMENT OF STATE

Mr. YEE. Thank you very much, Mr. Chairman. Chairman Rohrabacher, Representative Sires, members of the subcommittee, I want to thank you for inviting me and my colleague, Susan Fritz, to appear before you today to discuss the Western Balkans 20 years since the Dayton Accords were signed. We are deeply grateful to the Congress and this subcommittee, in particular, for your interest in the Western Balkans which are an integral part of our vision of a Europe, whole, free, and at peace. Your engagement with senior Balkan officials, both here and in the region has sent a powerful signal that the United States remains committed to the region's future.

Today that vision is more under threat than any time since the end of the Cold War. Russia's aggression in Ukraine and ISIL's reign of terror in Syria and Iraq have underlined the geostrategic importance of a strong, stable Europe including in the Western Balkans. In this new context, our work with Balkan partners to create a space for free markets and free peoples is more important than ever.

EU and NATO membership, aided by U.S. engagement and assistance remains the transformative political and economic force for the Western Balkans. Progress is happening. Albania and Croatia joined NATO in 2009. Croatia became the 28th EU member in 2013. Montenegro is making steady progress on EU accession negotiations and is intent on qualifying for NATO membership. Albania's recent elections were the best democratic transition in that country's history. Serbia and Kosovo are making landmark progress toward normalization. And lastly, Bosnia and Herzegovina has negotiated its EU Stabilization and Association Agreement. I would like to give just a quick update on the region's seven countries.

Bosnia and Herzegovina. Bosnia and Herzegovina remains one of the poorest countries in Europe and lags far behind the rest of the region in reforms needed for membership in the European Union and NATO. To catch up, Bosnia and Herzegovina will need to accelerate reforms. We and our European partners have urged Bosnia and Herzegovina to begin with socio-economic reforms that can make a tangible impact in the lives of Bosnia and Herzegovina citizens. These initial reforms must lead to institutional and political reforms that Bosnia and Herzegovina needs to become a stable, functional state, fully integrated with the rest of Europe. We believe that the future of Bosnia and Herzegovina lies in the EU and NATO, and like all other candidates Bosnia and Herzegovina will have to undertake substantial reform.

With the recent establishment of new state and entity-level governments that have reaffirmed their commitment to reform, we are hopeful the countries' leaders can deliver results.

Serbia. Serbia continues to improve relations with its neighbors and to build a stronger partnership with the European Union and the United states.

In January, Serbia assumed the chairmanship of the Organization for Security and Cooperation in Europe, the OSCE, and Serbia's leadership thus far has shown a strong commitment to supporting the organization's founding principles. We continue to support Serbia's aspirations to join the European Union and to commend Serbia's progress toward this goal.

Serbia has also recently taken steps to maintain constructive relations with neighbors, including Belgrade's hosting of Albanian Prime Minister Rama in November 2014, the first visit at that level between the two countries in 68 years. Most encouraging, Serbia's commitment to the EU-led Brussels dialogue with Kosovo has resulted in more normalized relationships, increased regional security, and mutual understanding.

Kosovo. Seven years after its declaration of independence, Kosovo has taken great strides to develop as a full sovereign, independent state. We continue to support Kosovo in its efforts to build a modern, multiethnic state with inclusive, democratic institutions. With the strong support of EU High Representative Mogherini, considerable progress on the Kosovo-Serbia dialogue has been made since both sides reconvened in February 2015, including with agreements to unify Kosovo's judicial system and to integrate the Kosovo-Serb Civilian Protection Corps into Kosovo institutions.

We also support the establishment of a Special Court to deal with the allegations contained in the 2011 Council of Europe report and urge Kosovo's leaders to take steps to approve the necessary legal framework.

Albania. Albania has seen significant democratic progress since the ending of oppressive communist rule 20 years ago. Last June, the European Council granted Albania EU country candidate status. In granting the status, the Council highlighted Albania's efforts at countering corruption and organized crime, and implementing judicial reform.

With over 1 year in office, the new government continues to hold Albania's strong partnership with the United States as a key strategic priority. We recently signed a U.S.-Albania strategic partnership, outlining key areas of cooperation, including security, rule of law, economic development and energy security. Nevertheless, much work lies ahead.

Despite receiving EU candidate status, Albania will face significant challenges implementing the reforms necessary for beginning EU accession talks.

Montenegro. Montenegro which began EU accession talks in June 2013 has come a long way. However, the European Union noted in October, a lack of credible investigations, prosecutions, and final convictions in corruption cases and serious concerns regarding freedom of expression and the media.

NATO has also urged Montenegro to strengthen the rule of law to improve its case for receiving an invitation to join NATO by the end of 2015. We agree with our NATO allies that no one outside the 28 member states, including Russia can interfere with or veto NATO's decisions on membership. We are also concerned about the relatively low level of Montenegrin public support for NATO membership, currently about 38 percent. Our hope is that Montenegro will accelerate the pace of its efforts and put its best case forward this year.

Macedonia. We support Macedonia's aspirations to join NATO and the European Union. Recently, however, we and our European partners have been following with concern the domestic political crisis in Macedonia related to the release of wiretap information by the head of the main opposition party. We are urging the government to address the leaked information in a way that demonstrates its commitment to Euro-Atlantic principles. We are encouraging the opposition which is currently boycotting Parliament to return to that body and help resolve the crisis. We are also concerned about a growing divide between the ethic-Macedonian majority and ethnic-Albanian minority communities.

Macedonia's integration into the EU and NATO remains important for achieving lasting peace and stability in the region. With a new government in Athens, we continue to urge both sides to arrive at a mutually acceptable solution to the so-called name issue which has blocked the country's Euro-Atlantic prospects.

Croatia. In July 2013, Croatia became the newest EU member and is now sharing lessons it learned with its neighbors who aspire to join the EU and NATO. Yet, challenges still lie ahead. The economy has contracted for the last 6 years, causing high unemployment and deterring further foreign investment. We encourage Croatia to take steps to improve the business climate, attract more investment and foster private sector led growth. Although much more work needs to be done, we welcome the recent tender for a business plan to develop the liquid natural gas, or LNG, terminal on Krk Island. The realization of this terminal will not only help Croatia reduce dependency on Russia or any other single source of gas, but also provide energy diversification for other central European countries who are much more dependent on Russian energy supplies.

Thank you, Mr. Chairman, Ranking Member Meeks, members of the subcommittee. I look forward to your questions.

[The prepared statement of Mr. Yee follows:]

Testimony by Deputy Assistant Secretary Hoyt Yee
House Foreign Affairs Committee, Subcommittee on Europe
"Achieving Peace and Stability in the Balkans: 20 years after the Dayton Accords"
April 29, 2015

Chairman Rohrabacher, Ranking Member Meeks, Members of the Subcommittee, thank you for inviting me to appear before you today to discuss what we have achieved in the western Balkans in the 20 years since the Dayton Accords and the challenges before us today. Let me express my deep gratitude to Congress and this Subcommittee for your interest in the western Balkans, where the United States is investing to complete our shared vision of a Europe that is whole, free, and at peace. Your engagement with senior Balkan officials, trips to the region and Caucus memberships have sent a powerful signal that the United States remains committed to the region's future.

Today that vision is more under threat than any time since the end of the Cold War. Russia's aggression in Ukraine and ISIL's reign of terror in Syria and Iraq have drawn the geostrategic importance of the western Balkans into high relief. In this new geopolitical context, our work with Balkans Allies and partners to create a space for free trade, free markets and free peoples is more important than ever – whether it's supporting the right to chart their own sovereign choice for a Euro-Atlantic future; cutting off the flow of foreign fighters to Syria and Iraq intent on sowing terror in the United States and Europe; shoring up the region's central role in Europe's energy security future; or rooting out the cancer of corruption eating away at livelihoods, democracies and security.

The appeal of EU and NATO membership—aided by U.S. engagement and assistance—has been a transformative political and economic force for the western Balkans. Progress is happening; Albania and Croatia joined the NATO in 2009; Croatia became the 28th EU member in 2013; Montenegro is making steady progress on EU accession negotiations and is in "Focused and Intensified Talks" this year to qualify for NATO membership; Albania's recent elections were the best democratic transition in that country's history; Serbia and Kosovo are making landmark progress toward normalization; and, lastly, Bosnia and Herzegovina has negotiated its EU Stabilization and Association Agreement.

Since 1990, the U.S. Government has provided over $7 billion to support these efforts through democratic reforms, focus on rule of law and counter-corruption efforts; aid the transition to market economies; advance post-conflict reconciliation; and support law enforcement in the fight against organized crime. But significant challenges remain. The Euro-Atlantic aspirations of many Western Balkan countries are still unfulfilled and threaten the progress that we've made in the 20 years since Dayton.

With this in mind, I would like to focus my testimony today on four key areas. First, I will provide a status update on the region's seven countries. Second, I will talk about the complex impact that Russian malign influence is having on the region. Third, I will explore our cooperation on counter-ISIL efforts, particularly how we are working together to effectively investigate and prosecute foreign terrorist fighters (FTF). Finally, I will examine the region's economic health.

Bosnia and Herzegovina

BiH remains one of the poorest countries in Europe and lags far behind the rest of the region in reforms needed for membership in the European Union and NATO. In order to catch up, BiH will need to accelerate reforms. We and our European partners have urged BiH to begin with socio-economic reforms that can make a tangible impact on the lives of BiH's citizens. We hope these initial reforms will lead to institutional and political reforms that BiH needs in order to become a stable, functional state fully integrated with the rest of Europe. We firmly believe that the future of BiH lies in the EU and NATO – and all new EU candidates have had to undertake substantial reform, including constitutional changes. BiH's constitution is based on the Dayton Accords, signed 20 years ago, and needs to be adapted to new facts and standards.

Key socio-economic reforms include labor law reform to enable a more dynamic jobs market, business climate reforms to streamline processes and cut red tape, and tax reforms to bring the costs of hiring in BiH more in line with EU standards. Public administration reform also has the potential to substantially improve the effectiveness of services, reduce costs to citizens through right-sizing, and unburden the private sector engine of the economy, which is right now held back by an overly cumbersome and exceptionally large public sector.

Outdated labor laws and collective bargaining agreements are difficult for any country to change, and are protected by entrenched interests – but the only way to create new jobs and growth is by modernizing the BiH economy. This includes overhauling state-owned companies that support a patronage system that favors political loyalty over professional competence. This corrupt system dooms these same state-owned enterprises to waste and mismanagement and has left some of them essentially bankrupt. Successful restructuring and privatization of these enterprises would make BiH's economy stronger, more competitive and able to create stable, well-paying jobs.

Corruption remains a serious problem in BiH. Our Embassy supports BiH's anti-corruption efforts in a variety of ways, including by working with police, judges, and prosecutors to strengthen capacity and help build cases related to corruption and organized crime. In addition to working with the government, we are also actively supporting civil society groups to advocate for transparency and protection for whistleblowers. Our goal is to help create an environment in which leaders and officials are held accountable for their actions and no one is above the law.

We also need to help foster a shared vision of the future for the citizens of Bosnia and Herzegovina. We saw the potential for this during the disastrous floods almost one year ago, when citizens came together as neighbors to meet the crisis. In the hour of need, rafting clubs, students, farmers and small business owners helped each other with no regard to ethnic background.

Serbia

Serbia continues to improve relations with neighbors, build a stronger partnership with the EU and United States, and cooperate in the international community on transnational threats.

In January, Serbia assumed the Chairmanship of the Organization for Security and Cooperation in Europe (OSCE), and Serbia's leadership thus far has shown a strong commitment to supporting the organization's founding principles. For example, Serbia has encouraged political discussion of the crisis within the OSCE and used the full toolbox of OSCE institutions and missions to support a peaceful resolution to the conflict. Recently, Serbia was successful in gaining an extension of the mandate of the Special Monitoring Mission in Ukraine until March 2016. We expect Serbia will continue as a transparent and judicious Chair, holding all participating States to the OSCE's high standards, in this fortieth anniversary year of the Helsinki Final Act. Foreign Minister Dacic's testimony here, before the Helsinki Commission in February 2015, is another indication of Serbia's readiness for dialogue and transparency.

We continue to support Serbia's aspirations to join the EU and commend Serbia's progress towards this goal. We welcome EU encouragement and assistance in support of reforms Serbia must take to bring itself in line with EU standards.

Serbia has been a NATO Partnership for Peace (PfP) member since 2006. We were pleased that after nearly four years of negotiations, Serbia completed in January its first-ever Individual Partnership Action Plan (IPAP) with NATO, which outlines a tailored set of programs for Serbian-NATO collaboration and opens a new chapter in Serbia's political relations with the Alliance. In addition, we applaud Serbia's increasing participation in global peacekeeping operations with the EU and UN in Africa and the Middle East, as well as Serbia's active participation in the multinational coalition against ISIL.

Serbian leaders have assured us they seek to strengthen regional stability and have constructive relations with all their neighbors. Several recent events have highlighted Serbia's commitment in this regard, including Belgrade's hosting of Albanian PM Rama in November 2014, the first visit at that level in 68 years, Serbian Prime Minister Vucic making his first trip abroad as Prime Minister in April 2014 to Sarajevo, and his participation in the February inauguration of the new Croatian president. Perhaps most encouraging, Serbia's commitment to the EU-led Brussels Dialogue with Kosovo has resulted in more normalized relations and concrete agreements that have increased regional security and understanding.

However, there also continue to be instances when Serbia refuses to participate in regional events in which Kosovo participates as the Republic of Kosovo. We have expressed our view that this policy of exclusion hinders dialogue and regional cooperation, and contributes to a negative image of the region, including to potential business investors. That said, we have seen promising steps recently. Today and tomorrow, in fact, Serbia is hosting a conference in Belgrade for regional Ministers of Interior – including from Kosovo – on combating the threat posed by foreign terrorist fighters. We welcome this inclusive approach.

Kosovo

Seven years after its declaration of independence and three years since the end of international supervision, Kosovo has taken great strides in its development as a fully sovereign, independent state. The United States continues to support Kosovo in its efforts to build a modern, multiethnic state with inclusive, democratic institutions.

The 2014 parliamentary elections in Kosovo were the first democratic transition of political authority resulting from free and fair elections held throughout all of Kosovo's territory. The coalition government and the process that led to its formation demonstrate the vitality of Kosovo's democratic and political institutions. We applaud President Jahjaga for her steadfast leadership during the transition to ensure Kosovo's laws and constitution were upheld.

We applaud the governments of Kosovo and Serbia on their continued commitment to the Brussels Agreement and normalization of relations through the EU-facilitated Dialogue. We fully support EU High Representative Mogherini's direct involvement. We congratulate all sides on the considerable progress made since they reconvened in February 2015, including agreements to unify Kosovo's judicial system and integrate the Kosovo Serb Civilian Protection Corps into Kosovo institutions. We encourage the EU and the governments of Kosovo and Serbia to maintain this momentum and implement agreements that will improve the lives of all of Kosovo's citizens.

We support the establishment of a Special Court to deal with the allegations contained in the 2011 Council of Europe report by Swiss Senator Marty and investigated by the Special Investigative Task Force. It is essential that Kosovo's leaders take the necessary steps to approve the constitutional amendments and legislation necessary for the creation of a Special Court that can address these allegations in a credible manner. It is important for the victims, but also for the future of Kosovo, to move beyond this chapter and continue its democratic consolidation and path toward Euro-Atlantic integration.

In addition to the United States, 106 other countries fully recognize Kosovo as a sovereign state. Kosovo is also a member of a number of regional and international organizations. The United States continues to actively encourage bilateral recognitions of Kosovo by engaging with non-recognizers at the highest levels whenever possible. We support Kosovo's eventual membership in NATO, the OSCE, and the European Union and encourage the government of Kosovo to adopt the reforms necessary to meet those institutions' standards.

Albania

In Albania, we have seen significant democratic progress since the ending of oppressive communist rule 20 years ago. Last June, the European Council granted Albania EU country candidate status. In granting this status, the European Council highlighted Albania's efforts at countering corruption, fighting organized crime, and implementing judicial reform.

With over one year under its belt in office, the new government continues to hold Albania's strong partnership with the United States as a key strategic priority. We recently signed a declaration of a U.S.-Albania Strategic Partnership, outlining areas of cooperation in security; good governance, rule of law, and human rights; civil society; economic development; energy security; and education and cultural exchanges.

Albania's economic growth rate ceased its decline in 2014, rebounding from 1.4 to 2 percent, due in part to a three-year IMF program, EU accession progress, headway in fighting corruption, improved government revenues, energy reform efforts, and increasing growth expectations. The IMF forecasts three percent economic growth in 2015, stimulated by foreign investment and a rebound in domestic demand. We continue to look for opportunities to help Albania create the conditions for broad-based, sustainable economic growth that are inclusive and aligned with EU standards.

Nevertheless, there remains much work ahead for Albania. Despite receiving country candidate status, Albania will face significant challenges implementing the reforms necessary for beginning EU accession talks. Albania will need to intensify efforts at strengthening democratic institutions, tackling judicial reform, and fighting corruption and organized crime. The influence of crime and corruption on politics is a continuing concern. We are urging the government and opposition to work together to fight crime and corruption, and not be distracted by confrontational and corrupt domestic politics.

Montenegro

Montenegro, which began EU accession talks only in June 2013, has come a long way. However, in the last EU Progress Report, issued in October, the EU noted that "a credible track record of investigations, prosecutions and final convictions in corruption cases, including high-level corruption, needs to be developed. Serious concerns remain with respect to freedom of expression and the media, including unresolved cases of violence against journalists."

NATO has also urged Montenegro to strengthen the rule of law to improve its case for receiving an invitation to join NATO by the end of 2015. We agree with our NATO Allies that no one outside the 28 member states, including Russia, has the right to interfere with or veto NATO's decisions on the membership issue. We are also concerned about the relatively low level of Montenegrin public support for NATO membership (currently about 38 percent), which largely stems from misconceptions about the responsibilities and benefits of membership.

We and other Allies continue to monitor and review Montenegro's reform progress and readiness for membership. We believe the Montenegrins are committed to implementing the reforms needed to demonstrate full readiness to join NATO. Our hope is that Montenegro keeps up or even accelerates the pace of its efforts and puts its best case forward this year.

Macedonia

We also support Macedonia's aspirations to join NATO and the EU. Recently, however, we and our European partners have been following with concern the domestic developments in Macedonia related to the release of wiretap information by the head of the main opposition party. We are continuing to encourage the opposition, which is currently boycotting Parliament, to return to that body and help resolve the crisis. We are also looking to the government to take action to resolve the crisis in a way that demonstrates its commitment to Euro-Atlantic principles, including rule of law, free and fair elections, and independence of the judiciary and the media. This is an opportunity to strengthen the capacity of existing institutions, to demonstrate Macedonia's ability to handle serious challenges and protect all citizens' rights, and to begin to rebuild public trust.

We are also concerned about a growing divide in society between the ethnic-Macedonian majority and ethnic-Albanian minority communities in Macedonia.

Macedonia's integration into the EU and NATO remains important for achieving lasting peace and stability in the region. At the 2008 Bucharest Summit, NATO pledged that Macedonia will receive an invitation to join the Alliance as soon as it agrees with Greece on a mutually acceptable solution to the name dispute. With a new government in Athens we continue to urge both sides to engage afresh, with a willingness to compromise.

The Government, the opposition and all involved must focus on the long-term strategic position of Macedonia, not on short-term tactical advantages.

Croatia

In Croatia, we have seen successive governments stick to an overarching goal – EU membership – to commit the resources and relentlessly pursue reforms needed to achieve it. The payoff came in July 2013 when Croatia became the newest EU member, demonstrating to the entire region that the door to EU integration is still open. We are very pleased to see that Zagreb is now sharing lessons it learned with its neighbors who aspire to join the EU and NATO.

There are still challenges that lie ahead for Croatia. First, their economy has contracted for the last six years, causing high employment and deterring further foreign direct investment. We have encouraged steps to promote reforms that could improve the business climate, attract more investment, and put momentum behind private-sector led economic growth. Second, until recently the Croatian government had not prioritized the liquefied natural gas (LNG) terminal project on Krk Island. We are encouraged by their recent tender for a business plan for the project. The realization of this LNG terminal would not only help Croatia remove any dependency on Russian gas, but also provide energy diversification for other central European countries who are much more dependent on Russian energy supplies.

Russian Malign Influence in the Western Balkans

Globally, the United States and Russia are cooperating on key security priorities such as countering violent extremism and the threat of foreign terrorist fighters, or in the Iran nuclear talks. We hope to achieve that same kind of cooperation in the western Balkans.

Given Russia's continued aggression in Ukraine, however, we remain watchful. We are fully committed to the Euro-Atlantic integration of the region and to supporting the aspirations in this regard of all the western Balkan countries. In contrast, since last September, Russian FM Lavrov said that NATO expansion in the western Balkans would be a provocative act. NATO continues to reiterate that it is a defensive Alliance, and not directed at any country, and does not pose a threat to Russia in any way. The countries of the region are and will remain free to determine their own associations, and Russia has no veto.

We are working to build regional resilience through our positive support of the region's NATO and EU integration goals.

On energy, where Russia has particular leverage in the region, we are working with western Balkan leaders and the EU to diversify supply sources, routes, and types so Russia cannot use its energy supplies as a political weapon, as it has done in Ukraine.

Foreign Terrorist Fighters

The western Balkans are a significant source of foreign terrorist fighters going to Syria and Iraq, particularly when considered as a per capita proportion of the population. BiH, Kosovo, Macedonia, and Albania in particular are notable source countries.

There is no one-size-fits-all profile of a foreign terrorist fighter from the western Balkans. Individuals are being radicalized and motivated to fight in Syria and Iraq by a number of factors. Economic stagnation and lack of employment options are factors. This is compounded by skepticism of citizens about their governments.

The western Balkan countries are taking this threat very seriously – Albania, BiH, Kosovo, Macedonia, Montenegro, and Serbia have all passed legislation criminalizing foreign fighters and support for them. The U.S. is providing significant assistance through technical advice, training in capacity building in terrorism cases and legislative strengthening. In addition, the U.S. has recently placed a U.S. prosecutor in the Embassy in Tirana as a Counterterrorism Resident Legal Adviser with regional responsibilities.

Albania, BiH, Kosovo, and Serbia have all arrested suspected foreign fighters and are in the process of investigating and prosecuting them. The U.S. is providing case based mentoring in Albania, BiH and Kosovo to assist investigators and prosecutors to effectively prosecute their cases.

Economy of the Western Balkans

25 years after independence, the western Balkans are making steady progress towards Euro-Atlantic integration, but much work remains, particularly regarding their economies. Countries remain stuck in transition, with unemployment averaging over 20 percent (and more than double this among youth), out-sized public sectors, large informal sectors, and rigid labor laws that just now are being re-written to allow for more dynamic job markets. GDP in the region has grown only 10 percent from its 1989 level. Wars in the 1990s and the 2008 financial crisis had their obvious effects, but there have been successes and the region's trajectory toward the West and free-market capitalism remains.

Foreign direct investment is particularly important for the region's economic success, in light of its small national markets and persistently high unemployment. In the five years before the financial crisis, the region averaged annual GDP growth of over 5 percent with impressive foreign direct investment inflows that represented 25 percent of Montenegro's GDP in 2007, for example.

Significant job growth, particularly among youth, and a burgeoning middle class are critical for increased economic security, shared prosperity, and eventual EU accession. Together with international partners we are advocating business-friendly and growth-oriented structural reforms, legislation, and investments needed to attract businesses and transition the region's economies to more competitive, private-sector driven models of growth. Firms need to have confidence that contracts will be respected, goods will clear customs quickly, permits will be issued in a transparent and timely manner, and labor rights are respected.

Examples of recent progress include Serbia, which adopted in 2014 several business climate reforms that were drafted with U.S. technical assistance and policy support; and Albania, where we are providing technical assistance to the electricity sector and advisory services to the government as it upgrades and restructures the sector.

More broadly on energy, which plays a fundamental role in any economy, we are supporting the region's integration into Europe's energy markets, and providing options to diversify supply sources, supply routes, and energy mixes in order to increase countries' energy security. We are encouraging adoption of EU rules on competition and third party access to energy infrastructure to increase competition and make the energy sector more attractive for foreign investment.

Conclusion

What I have laid out are just a few of the numerous challenges western Balkans countries face in strengthening economies, opening new opportunities for growth and development, and building multi-ethnic democracies. The United States and its European partners will continue to assist these countries in any way that we can to implement the reforms necessary to tackle these challenges, particularly those impeding progress on their Euro-Atlantic paths. While our commitment to helping create a brighter future is unwavering, it should be clear to all that the ultimate responsibility for adhering to the path of reform and integration rests with the region's elected leaders. Citizens and civil societies must be prepared to hold their governments accountable when they stray from the path or stall along the way.

Thank you again for the opportunity to testify before the Committee.

Mr. ROHRABACHER. Thank you very much. We have been joined by Mr. Meeks and with your permission, Mr. Meeks, I will have Ms. Fritz' testimony and then you will be able to give your opening statement, etcetera.

STATEMENT OF MS. SUSAN FRITZ, ACTING ASSISTANT ADMINISTRATOR, EUROPE AND EURASIA BUREAU, U.S. AGENCY FOR INTERNATIONAL DEVELOPMENT

Ms. FRITZ. Thank you, Mr. Chairman, Chairman Rohrabacher, Ranking Member Meeks, and Congressman Sires. I want to thank you for the opportunity to appear before you today, along with my colleague, Hoyt Yee, to discuss USAID's assistance and priorities in the Balkans

The mission of the U.S. Agency for International Development is to partner to end extreme poverty and promote resilient, democratic societies while advancing our security and prosperity. In the Balkans, USAID has played a key role since the breakup of Yugoslavia, helping raise standards of living and assisting countries on their path toward Euro-Atlantic integration and to becoming more tolerant, stable, and democratic societies. USAID is committed and focused on how we build on this momentum to address the serious remaining challenges as part of a coordinated U.S. Government strategy. Corruption, democratic drift, fragile economies, and uncertain domestic political climates all threaten the gains made since the Dayton Accords were signed 20 years ago.

Today, I would like to build on Deputy Assistant Secretary Hoyt Yee's updates on the five individual countries where USAID continues to work with a particular focus on how our programs have impacted some of the foreign policy priorities DAS Yee mentioned, such as preventing violent extremism, supporting governments and societies in becoming more stable and resilient to potentially detrimental external influences, and strengthening the region's economic health.

USAID's longstanding role in the Balkans and across Europe and Eurasia is to work with host countries, civil society, private sector and international partners to build the institutions of government, the economic systems, and the free civil societies that lead to democracy and prosperity. Our job is to help build the foundations of ''a Europe Whole, Free, and at Peace.''

Let me highlight a few examples of our democracy and governance activities in the region. In Bosnia and Herzegovina, USAID's assistance to Parliament staff and members has helped them to complete their legally mandated budget process which includes public debates on priorities and impact analyses, leading to more functional and accountable institutions across the entire government that better meet the needs of the citizens.

In Serbia and Kosovo, our activities have strengthened rule of law by improving the independence, transparency, efficiency and professionalism of the judiciary. Our anti-corruption assistance in Serbia has been pivotal to increasing the transparency and overall capacity of key independent agencies to execute their mandates.

In Macedonia, USAID's media program has increased the legitimacy of independent media and strengthened freedom of expression by promoting investigative journalism and establishing a media fact-checking service which has published online more than a thousand peer reviews of media articles.

In Albania, USAID is providing assistance to strengthen local government accountability, financing and services including the crafting of a fiscal decentralization framework and a critical law for the structuring of local government. In the economic sphere, USAID programs in the Balkans are bolstering entrepreneurs as well, as the laws and policies have let them thrive in stable financial systems.

We help governments to establish energy policies, to diversify supplies, and connect to European markets, increasing safe, clean power for industry and citizens.

Let me highlight a few examples of our economic growth efforts. In Bosnia, USAID's assistance and loan guarantees, particularly to small agribusinesses is helping to increase sales and exports. Our Farmer Project, for example, reported increased sales for companies assisted by USAID of 54 percent over 4 years. USAID helped the Albanian Government to achieve critical reports in the energy market, resulting in the electricity company saving $75 million last year through implementation of practical loss reduction techniques that were provided by our advisors.

USAID's critical support to Kosovo's Government to unbundle electricity distribution and supply enabled it to privatize the Kosovo Energy Corporation resulting in improved infrastructure investment, billing and collections, reducing technical and commercial losses.

In Macedonia, we are helping streamline laws and regulations for clean, renewable energy to promote more investment in the sector. We have also expanded access to finance for small and medium businesses.

In Serbia, USAID assistance was instrumental in reforming Serbia's labor law, reducing the burdens of its inspection system and is modernizing its outdated construction permitting system.

USAID is working to improve the competitiveness of the private sector, especially economically disadvantaged regions populated by ethnic minorities.

Mr. Chairman, since Dayton, the Balkan countries have made remarkable progress in the reforms needed to further integrate into Euro-Atlantic institutions and to build resilient democracies. With that said, we know that our work in this region is far from done. We recognize, as you have pointed out, that there has been political and economic stagnation in the region. The Balkan countries where USAID works, Albania, Macedonia, Kosovo, Serbia, and Bosnia and Herzegovina need continued U.S. engagement and attention.

We look forward to working with you and your colleagues in Congress to strengthen U.S. engagement and more specifically, USAID's activities in the Balkans to build on the progress that has been made to achieve our goal of a Europe, free, whole and at peace.

Thank you again and I look forward to your questions.

[The prepared statement of Ms. Fritz follows:]

Written Testimony by USAID Acting Assistant Administrator for Europe and Eurasia
Susan Fritz
House Foreign Affairs Committee, Subcommittee on Europe, Eurasia and Emerging
Threats
"Progress and Challenges in the Western Balkans"
April 29, 2015

Chairman Rohrabacher, Ranking Member Meeks, Members of the Subcommittee, I want to thank you for the opportunity to appear before you today, along with my colleague Hoyt Yee, to discuss USAID's assistance and priorities in the Balkans.

The mission of the U.S. Agency for International Development is to partner to end extreme poverty and promote resilient, democratic societies while advancing our security and prosperity. In the Balkans, USAID has played a key role since the breakup of Yugoslavia, helping raise standards of living and assisting countries on their path towards Euro-Atlantic integration and to becoming more tolerant, stable, and democratic societies. We have made a lot of progress and USAID is committed and focused on how we build on this momentum to address the serious remaining challenges as part of a coordinated U.S. government strategy. Corruption, democratic drift, fragile economies, and uncertain domestic political climates all threaten the gains made since the Dayton Accords were signed 20 years ago.

Today I would like to build on Deputy Assistant Secretary Hoyt Yee's updates on the five individual countries where USAID continues to work, with a particular focus on how our programs have impacted some of the foreign policy priorities DAS Yee mentioned – such as preventing violent extremism, supporting governments and societies in becoming more stable and resilient to potentially detrimental external influences, and strengthening the region's economic health.

USAID's longstanding role in the Balkans and across Europe and Eurasia is to work with host countries and international partners to build the institutions of government, the economic systems, and the free civil societies that lead to democracy and prosperity. Our job is to help build the foundations of "a Europe Whole, Free, and at Peace."

Over the past two decades, USAID's programs in the Balkans have been designed to accelerate democratic progress and European integration. Today we partner with governments, civil society and other donors in Kosovo, Bosnia and Herzegovina, Albania, Serbia, and Macedonia to strengthen democracies and the rule of law, confront endemic corruption, and expand civil society and a free press.

In the economic sphere, USAID programs are bolstering entrepreneurs, as well as the laws and policies that will let them thrive in stable financial systems. We help governments to establish energy policies to diversify supplies and connect to European markets, increasing safe, clean power for industry and citizens. Programs like these show citizens in the region a path to a more prosperous future.

Mr. Chairman, since Dayton the Balkan countries have made remarkable progress in the reforms needed to further integrate into Euro-Atlantic institutions and to build resilient democracies. With that said, we know that our work in this region is far from done – we recognize -- as you have pointed out -- that there has been political and economic stagnation in some areas of the region. While a few nations graduated relatively quickly from USAID assistance, including Croatia and Slovenia, and some such as Serbia continue to progress, the Balkan countries where USAID works—Albania, Macedonia, Kosovo, Serbia, and Bosnia-Herzegovina— need sustained U.S engagement and attention. We look forward to working with you and your colleagues in Congress to strengthen U.S. engagement and more specifically USAID's activities in the Balkans to build on the progress that has been made to achieve our goal of "a Europe Whole, Free, and at Peace."

Next I will highlight USAID's strategy and a few programs in each country.

Bosnia and Herzegovina

The Dayton Peace Accords brought an end to the 1992-95 war and began the transition to peace and stability in Bosnia and Herzegovina. Today, physically, the country is largely rebuilt and shows signs of economic growth. The European Union recently agreed to bring Bosnia's Stabilization and Association Agreement into force in June, the first step in the process for pursuing EU membership. Yet development continues to be hindered by ethnic tensions and a largely dysfunctional, multi-layered bureaucracy, which while intended to safeguard the rights of the various ethnic groups, has been manipulated by Bosnia's politicians to protect their narrow interests and stymie political and economic progress.

USAID's objective is to help Bosnia meet its commitments to join the European Union, providing support for economic, democratic, and social progress in Bosnia and Herzegovina.

- High unemployment is a fundamental challenge that is an obstacle for countries like Bosnia to joining the European Union. Our technical experts focus on agriculture, agribusiness, and on tourism, and on unlocking the potential of Bosnia's energetic diaspora. Our "FARMA" project, for example, reported increased sales for companies assisted by USAID of 54% over four years. Our loan guarantee programs with commercial banks unlock much-needed financial capital. USAID helps Bosnia improve its economic governance through better fiscal coordination and compliance at all levels of government; establish a more transparent, modern system of direct taxation and collection of social benefits to create a more business-friendly environment; and advance reforms in the financial sector and strengthen audit capacity.

- USAID helps municipal governments and private businesses capitalize on economic potential and opportunities at the local level. The assistance will result in domestic and foreign direct investment, more competitive local industry, especially for small and medium-sized enterprises. USAID projects help connect producers to markets and introduce new technologies along the entire value chain. This includes assistance in marketing Bosnia and Herzegovina as a tourist destination and helping local producers meet EU quality and safety standards in agriculture. USAID works to reform energy policy to help Bosnia to maximize its potential as a net energy exporter.

- USAID's democracy and governance assistance helps Bosnia and Herzegovina to develop more functional and accountable institutions with increased citizen participation in political and social decision making. To combat corruption, USAID supported a two-year civic advocacy campaign. Leadership for the campaign was provided by the Center for Responsible Democracy Luna, USAID partner Centers for Civic Initiatives, and NGO members of USAID's anti-corruption network, ACCOUNT. Civil society, a multi-party group of parliamentarians, and representatives of BiH institutions worked together to draft and adopt the legislation, a joint effort that set an example of how the government and NGOs can work together and address major issues that affect citizens' lives. Corruption costs approximately $1 billion every year, money that could be used for building roads and schools. The result is like imposing a direct tax of $275 (400 BAM) per year on every man, woman and child in BiH.

- USAID projects provide technical assistance to all levels of governments—ministries, lawmakers and parliamentary committees—to enhance public engagement on policy development and improve accountability in budget planning, implementation and oversight. USAID assists elected representatives to develop, draft, advocate and implement legislation and improve their responsiveness and accountability to their constituents. USAID strengthens legal systems to provide transparent access to justice for all citizens. Finally, USAID is implementing the country's most significant nationwide effort at promoting community reconciliation and reducing ethnic tension.

- USAID assisted the State and the Federation Members of Parliament and the staff of four committees in completing their legally mandated ten-step budget cycle. USAID facilitated public debates on expenditure policy and priorities, the budget framework, and an analysis for the final budget proposal before its adoption in 2014. This was the first time that committee members provided justification for new budget appropriations, stated their objectives and expected results, conducted a value for the money analysis, and analyzed the gender implications for their proposed allocations.

- Youth, reconciliation, and women's empowerment are priorities across all USAID programs in Bosnia and Herzegovina. USAID supports youth and women to increase their civic and economic opportunities, to become responsible and productive citizens, and to become involved in and integrally a part of the country's future. Reconciliation is a sub-component of many USAID programs in Bosnia and Herzegovina, bringing together different ethnic communities to work on shared economic and democratic objectives.

Serbia

USAID's programs in Serbia have the overall strategic goal of supporting Serbia in its vision to be democratic, prosperous and fully integrated into Euro-Atlantic institutions. Since 2001, USAID has assisted to stimulate economic growth, strengthen the justice system, and promote good governance in Serbia.

Despite having gained European Union (EU) candidate status in March 2012 and opening accession negotiations in January 2014, Serbia's current reform path is not yet irreversible. Although Serbia's current government is focused on EU integration, domestic public enthusiasm for EU membership is not always steadfast, and our programs play a key role in keeping Serbia's reform momentum moving forward.

Serbia's economy is constrained by critical barriers to growth—particularly in its business enabling environment. The private sector needs to increase its ability to compete in international markets, and jobs are needed to combat high unemployment, especially in vulnerable communities.

USAID's programs work to address both democratic governance and sustained economic growth while building the capacity of key counterparts at the national and local levels to move the country toward lasting political and economic stability.

- USAID support has produced a more professional and financially viable independent media.

- Activities strengthen Serbia's rule of law by improving the independence, transparency, efficiency, and professionalism of the Serbian judiciary.

- Anti-corruption assistance increases the capacity of key independent agencies to execute their mandates.

- USAID strengthens the sustainability of civil society organizations and their ability to interact with and oversee the government.

- USAID supports the Government of Serbia's efforts to implement program-based budgeting and to integrate this methodology into the country's national strategic planning process.

- USAID works with selected government counterparts, non-governmental organizations, international donors, and other U.S. agencies to advance economic reforms that will contribute to business growth, to strengthen the capacity of municipalities to stimulate local economic development by better meeting the needs of businesses and the market.

- USAID is working to improve the competitiveness of the private sector, especially in economically disadvantaged regions populated by ethnic minorities.

- USAID assistance was instrumental in reforming Serbia's labor law, reducing the burden of its inspections system, and modernizing its outdated construction permitting system.

Kosovo

In 1999 Kosovo was a war-torn territory lacking the basic institutions needed to govern. In the last 14 years the country has achieved many successes, including statehood. It has developed institutions, undertaken necessary institutional reform, and gone through the process of decentralization. Kosovo has made significant progress in building key ministries and government bodies that now have well-established and strong foundations.

Despite all of these achievements, judicial independence and the rule of law remain weak. Continuing inefficiencies in the system prevent the judicial branch from effectively playing its role as a counterbalance to the powerful executive branch. Members of the national legislature (Assembly of Kosovo) have limited autonomy, and the political landscape remains dominated by the executive branch and political party leaders. Kosovo remains the poorest economy in the region and struggles with high levels of poverty, staggering unemployment, and an overdependence on imports.

USAID's goal in Kosovo is increasing prosperity, integration within the Euro-Atlantic community, with more effective and accountable governance. Since 1999, USAID assistance has been committed to the reconstruction of Kosovo and to building self-governing institutions and a viable economy.

The current Government of Kosovo appears committed to leading and implementing reforms, providing USAID with an opening to engage in policy dialogue around key reform issues and to focus the welcomed assistance in a number of key areas:

- USAID is helping to strengthen a transparent, independent, and accountable judiciary through implementation of laws, oversight, management, and increased professional skills.

- USAID is assisting the Kosovo government to promote and support sound governance across the economic landscape, not only through better implementation of reforms but also by improving public financial management, increasing access to credit, attracting foreign investment, and increasing private sector participation in building public infrastructure and providing public services.

- Since Kosovo's population is mainly farm-based, USAID will continue its engagement in the agriculture sector, focusing on increasing the volume and productivity of high-value crops. USAID's support to agriculture in Kosovo resulted in increased sales of fresh and processed products. The most recently completed USAID agricultural activity that ended in December 2014 improved technologies, expanded and diversified production, and developed new market linkages.

- On September 26, 2012 a USAID loan guarantee agreement was signed between USAID Development Credit Authority (DCA) and six local commercial banks with funding from the Kosovo Ministry of Agriculture, Forestry and Rural Development (MAFRD). From €2.5 million ($3.1 million) gifted from MAFRD to USAID for loan subsidies, $26 million in loans will be generated. This is the first time in the history of DCA's loan guarantee program that a government counterpart completely covered the subsidy costs of a guarantee. As of November 2014, 650 loans were issued with terms ranging from 12- 48 months with an average loan size of $23,000. A total of $15 million in loans was disbursed, issued to enterprises in various agribusiness sectors such as dairy, livestock, animal feed, fruits and vegetables and other related sub-sectors. The loan guarantee is also changing banking behavior. Banks now are hiring and training dedicated agro-lending experts who understand how to structure loans to the agricultural sector.

- Technical experts from USAID are assisting with the reform of commercial law, property rights, and alternative dispute resolution mechanisms.

- A recently signed contract launched a transformational public-private partnership (PPP) for the Brezovica ski resort complex in Kosovo. This PPP illustrates the effectiveness of U.S. development assistance. USAID transaction advisors played a vital role bringing the landmark deal to closure. The $460 million investment is the largest in Kosovo's history and will create over 3,000 direct jobs and thousands of additional jobs in related sectors (construction, tourism, agriculture). The Brezovica ski resort is located in a predominantly ethnic-Serb area, and as an economic asset has strong relevance for Kosovo, the Kosovo-Serbia normalization dialogue, and for creating a thriving multi-ethnic society with opportunities for all in Kosovo.

- USAID is assisting the National and Municipal Assemblies to communicate with and respond to citizens' concerns.

- USAID is also assisting municipal administrations to improve accountability, especially in the areas of financial management and the development of own-source revenue.

- With the aim of initiating and supporting Kosovo's first business arbitration services, the Mission funded Alternative Dispute Resolution Centers at the Kosovo Chamber of Commerce (KCC) and the American Chamber of Commerce (AmCham). In FY 2014, the KCC registered seven arbitration cases and continued outreach activities and arbitration training. The KCC has calculated that, in its first year of operation, it will receive $128,321 in administrative fees, nearly matching the original $150,000 award from USAID. Meanwhile, the AmCham Alternative Dispute Resolution Center continued providing training to businesses in alternative dispute resolution mechanisms and concluded MoUs with four local universities to organize Legal Clinics in Arbitration.

- USAID's critical support to Kosovo's government to unbundle electricity distribution and supply enabled it to privatize the Kosovo Energy Corporation, resulting in improved infrastructure investment, billing and collections, and reduced technical and commercial losses. The newly formed Kosovo Electricity Distribution and Supply Company (KEDS) has largely met its pledges with investments to improve the grid system, replace old meters, and improve billing and collections, which have reached 95% (greater than the target set by the energy regulator) before social cases (families unable to pay their electricity bill) are considered. KEDS has also made significant strides towards reducing technical and commercial losses. By more effectively negotiating when tendering for imported electricity, KEDS has reduced the cost of imports, on average, by 16%, with significant downward pressure on future electricity tariffs.

- USAID is providing scholarships opportunities for young Kosovo citizens, mostly at the Master's Degree level, in targeted sectors that are aligned with the country's most pressing needs for skilled professionals.

Albania

Albania is the only Western Balkan country that wasn't part of former Yugoslavia, and has a unique institutional history and divergent development path. Overall progress since the transition on both governance and economic growth has been very dramatic. The pace of reforms slowed after initial steep gains, and Albania now grapples with many of the same challenges faced by its neighbors.

Albania struggles with poor service provision, an unstable civil service with relatively weak administrative capacity, and a myriad of rule of law challenges. A recently passed territorial reform will consolidate Albania's more than 300 existing local government districts into some 65 larger districts, which will help give local administrations the critical mass and human capital to enhance local government capabilities.

Albania has been hit hard by the weakness of the economy in southern Europe, with main trading partners in Greece and Italy suffering recession. The domestic market is small, and the two main drivers of previous economic growth, remittances and construction, have slowed dramatically. Weak contract enforcement hurts prospects of foreign direct investment. Bright spots in the Albanian economy are light manufacturing, tourism and agriculture, which have been flagged by the government as key priorities.

In Albania, USAID's strategic objective is to bolster prospects for European integration by focusing on good governance and inclusive economic growth. Throughout our portfolio, we strengthen capacities and incentives for citizen engagement with government.

In Albania, as in other Western-Balkan countries, USAID works closely with EU member states to leverage our impact, both in dollar terms as well as in policy reforms. USAID is working with emerging EU donors such as Slovenia to leverage funds and improve institutional and market linkages. Utilizing our extensive in-country expertise, a key point of strength for USAID, we are able to stretch taxpayer resources further.

Some of the specific activities in which we are currently engaged in Albania include:

- USAID is providing assistance to strengthen the accountability, financing, and service outcomes of local government, including the crafting of a fiscal decentralization framework and a critical law for the structuring of local government.

- To make courtrooms more efficient and transparent, USAID's program to strengthen the justice sector has assisted in the introduction of audio recording for all court sessions in every courtroom at district and appellate levels, and in "first instance" and "serious crimes" courts, reaching a total of 30 courts. Better court reporting promotes transparency, fairness, and efficiency; bolsters the watchdog and anticorruption roles of civil society organizations and the media; and strengthens the legal profession and legal education. The program is part of ongoing US support to the rule of law in Albania with an emphasis on improving justice delivery and realizing public demand for accountability in the justice sector.

- USAID recognizes the clear linkages between rule of law and the economy, and our justice sector work is aimed squarely at improving the transparency and efficiency of the courts.

- USAID has assisted Albania in achieving critical reforms in the energy market. Utilizing practical loss-reduction techniques recommended by USAID, the electricity distribution company was able to save $75 million dollars in 2014 alone and introduce real market discipline. This will save natural resources and strengthen energy independence.

- USAID has been very effective at helping Albanian farmers access capital, both from the private sector and from European Union sources. For every dollar invested, we can demonstrate $12 mobilized, and despite modest funding we have achieved macro-level impacts in agriculture in terms of exports and investments.

- Building on the successful, multi-sectoral collaboration between the U.S. and Sweden in Bosnia and Herzegovina, we will soon launch a joint program in Albania aimed at promoting growth in areas with high employment potential, particularly tourism.

Macedonia

While Macedonia has clearly made progress towards EU accession in the past, more recently some worrying signs have emerged. The opposition party continues to boycott the Parliament. Divisions between ethnic Albanians and ethnic Macedonians, which were exacerbated by the 2001 conflict, have become more acute. While political pluralism continues to exist in limited ways, challenges to citizens' engagement and participation in governance, and government accountability appear to have increased recently.

USAID's strategic objective in Macedonia -- a democratic, educated, prosperous state that responds to the needs of all of its citizens -- supports the full integration of Macedonia into Euro-Atlantic institutions. To reach this goal, USAID assistance focuses on creating greater checks and balances among the three branches of the government, strengthening the education system so that youth are better prepared to enter the modern workforce, and increasing job-creating private sector growth.

USAID's assistance over the years has greatly contributed to the progress that Macedonia has made towards EU accession. USAID assistance has also substantially supported Macedonia's transition to a market-based, competitive economy. We have improved the business environment to promote investment in the private sector. We have promoted economic sectors such as the dairy industry and adventure tourism that have the potential to increase employment and incomes for Macedonia's workers and small businesses. Ethnic integration in education is a particular problem given that the requirement that children be educated in their native languages has led to de facto school segregation.

Here are some of the specific activities in which we are involved:

- USAID established a reliable system for enforcement of court decisions reducing the average time for enforcement from 340 to 60 days.

- Over the past two years, USAID's media program has increased the legitimacy of independent media and strengthened freedom of expression by promoting investigative journalism and establishing a media fact checking service, which published online more than 1,000 peer reviews of media articles.

- Through our support the National Entrepreneurship and Competitiveness Council was re-launched in 2014 to improve public-private dialogue on government economic and business policies and regulations.

- We're helping Macedonia to streamline laws and regulations for clean, renewable energy investments to promote more investment in this sector.

- We've expanded access to finance for small and medium-size businesses.

- USAID's Anti-corruption Project, implemented by the local NGO Macedonian Center for International Cooperation, has supported the formation of a coalition of like-minded CSOs that are ready and able to hold institutions accountable with a unified voice. The Anti-Corruption Coalition on March 25th issued a joint statement calling for the relevant institutions to act within thirty days on the alleged malpractices, unlawful treatment, corruption and violation of human rights that have recently come to light.

- Nearly 20% of Macedonians make their living from agriculture or agriculture-related business, yet farming in Macedonia is plagued with inefficiency. By introducing drip irrigation to Macedonia's dairy farmers, USAID's Grow More Corn initiative is increasing corn production and enhancing economic growth as well. What started two years ago with 40 farmers, each demonstrating the power of drip irrigation on one hectare, is now a true phenomenon in Macedonia's agricultural sector. Yields on the demonstration fields soared from anemic to record-breaking numbers in one season and the results have piqued the interest of farmers, dairy processors, bankers, other international donors, and recalibrated the management of Macedonia's agricultural subsidy program.

- USAID has fostered over 260 partnerships between mono-ethnic schools and establishing School Integration Teams in all of the country's schools. As a result, students from different ethnic groups have had the opportunity to participate in joint student projects, excursions, performances, and sport activities, helping to reduce stereotypes and prevent conflict. USAID has partnered with the Department of Defense (through the European Command) to renovate over 40 schools, encouraging school and community participation in ethnic integration activities and helping over 20,000 students to have warmer, safer learning environments. In addition to the $770,000 that the Ministry of Education has contributed to these renovation efforts, municipalities have provided, on average, 30% of the cost of each school renovation.

- USAID's E-Accessibility project helps schools in Macedonia to mainstream their disabled students. A survey revealed that more than 80 percent of schools had at least one student with special educational needs, yet fewer than 20 percent of schools had an accessible entrance ramp, and the use of assistive computer peripherals and accessibility software were virtually unknown. Since 2010, USAID's e-Accessible Education Project has provided assistive computer peripherals and accessible educational software to 33 schools.

Region-wide

Throughout the Western Balkans, our Missions have moved purposely and aggressively in working directly with local implementers. Partnerships with local organizations ensure buy-in, enhance sustainability, and leverage the enormous clout that the United States, and USAID in particular, has in E&E countries.

- In Albania, 50% of the implementing mechanisms are through local organizations.

- In Bosnia. 38% of the implementing mechanisms are through local organizations.

- Approximately 41% of USAID Macedonia's FY 2014 budget was implemented directly by local NGOs. As a result of the Mission's continued efforts to promote local professional talent, 23 of the 27 projects employ local Chiefs of Party and key personnel.

- Serbia has signed six grants to local NGOs and launched a competition for additional local direct grants. Through this competition the Mission expects to make another seven awards to local NGOs.

- The United States has supported the Regional Housing Program, a multi-donor trust fund with $20 million since FY12, via support from the State Department's Bureau for Population, Refugees, and Migration (PRM). The program is providing housing solutions in Serbia, Bosnia and Herzegovina, Croatia, and Montenegro to vulnerable refugees and internally displaced persons (IDPs who lost their homes during the wars of the early 90's. Additional PRM support through NGOs is helping bulnerable refugees and displaced persons across the region, including in Kosovo, to access legal services and livelihood activities, and is facilitating community integration for ethnic minorities returning to their homes.

- Let me also highlight our regional Investigative Journalism activity. With a USAID investment of just over $3 million over four years, the Organized Crime and Corruption Reporting Project (OCCRP) has published groundbreaking stories that have helped provide the basis significant number of fines, asset freezes or cash seizures. Based on the stories broken by OCCRP, a conservative estimate of $562 million in illicit funds have been seized, frozen, or fined.

Programs like these, developed and executed in partnership with national and local governments, international partners, and citizens themselves, are moving the Balkans toward Europe.

Thank you again. I look forward to questions.

Mr. ROHRABACHER. We have had two very optimistic pieces of testimony here.

Mr. Meeks, would you like to have an opening statement? And then you may also proceed with any questions that you have for the witnesses.

Mr. MEEKS. Thank you, Mr. Chairman, and I want to thank you for holding this hearing to provide us with the status update on the Western Balkans region and I look forward to working with you in this 114th Congress on this region and as we have been talking about look forward to visiting this region soon so that we can go and see for ourselves what is going on on the ground.

With the West's attention justifiably being attracted to the Ukraine and related issues, we must not forget the importance and the delicate state of progress in the Western Balkans and I am encouraged by this hearing on the region to reaffirm our stance support for its peaceful and prosperous future.

Today's hearing is for me an opportunity to examine the tough issues and potential for advancements for a region that has a lot of promise. The quagmire of the Balkan Wars of the 1990s gives us a reference point for today's hearing. As the region spiraled into chaos, the United States and NATO led an international effort to put an end to the killing. The war set the region back in its move toward democracy and free-market capitalization and continued to haunt its citizens and policy makers. Western thinkers tend to present the Western Balkans' history and current events through two different lenses in my opinion, one that reckons that outside involvement played the leading role in getting us to the wars and consequently the current situation, while the other claims that the fate of Yugoslavia was doomed regardless of what outsiders did.

In today's hearing, I would like to argue the role of the Balkan people themselves who are often dismissed in these discussions. As much as recently written histories and international bodies affect the current situations here, it is the decisions of local politicians, businesses, and citizens that will definitely decide where this region will go. It is up to us and Congress to support healthy democratic, economic, and peaceful progress on the ground. We, the United States, have invested billions of dollars and many lives in order to ensure peace and prosperity in the region. The people there who have sacrificed more deserved it. In fact, there are signs of promise across the region. The regions are over a decade without armed conflict. Croatia, a reliable NATO partner, joined the EU in July 2013. And Serbia is technically on track to follow suit later this decade.

Freedom House named Kosovo, an electoral democracy for the first in their 2015 report. Montenegro recently passed substantial reforms to the rule of law and the defense and intelligent sectors, taking it closer to NATO membership. These are all encouraging steps in the right direction that should be recognized and supported.

Nevertheless, change is rarely linear and we will examine the breaks that impede progress as they apply to specific states. Sluggish economic growth, continuing problems in the fight against corruption, and serious questions with regard to the rule of law beset the region with an undertow pulling against the progress that had been made.

How can Congress support regional actors in combating these forces? And what about the EU? How much progress can be made without a bold accession strategy from the regional power, the EU. Ensuring the success of the region's development and encouraging democratic progress is of strategic importance to the United States and our interest are critically linked.

So I hope, as I have heard some of the testimony already, the opinions on this fascinating region, the leaders of the governments there should know that we are concerned with the state of affairs and after this hearing we look forward to following up on what is discussed. The fragile piece of the region is one that we, together with our EU partners must work hard at and encouraging.

I look forward to a fruitful discussion and questions that we can explore what Congress can offer and do to help to ensure economic growth, equality and peace for all in the region.

Thank you for giving me that opportunity, Mr. Chairman.

Mr. ROHRABACHER. If you would like to go straight to questions, we will let you go first.

Mr. MEEKS. Let me first deal first with whole piece on EU accession. And some said, the European Union has lost its magic in the sense, but not its importance in the region. And they fault EU expansion fatigue or the lack of progress on the part of the countries applying to join, but the EU integration process has definitely slowed.

One could question the specific state of accession in each Western Balkan country, but how do you assess the progress as a whole and the trends associated with it?

Mr. Yee?

Mr. YEE. Thank you, Representative Meeks, for that question and for your comments. I believe the European Union remains committed to enlarging the Union and to fulfill its commitment to the Western Balkans to continue to integrate all the countries of the Western Balkans as part of the European project.

I would agree with you, Representative Meeks, that the process has slowed. I think this is clearly a dynamic process in which on both sides there are requirements. On the European Union side the Union, the members of the Union want to be sure that by adding new members they will be, in fact, strengthening the Union, not weakening it, and that the members, the countries which are aspiring to membership are truly ready to meet all of the obligations including economic, as well as political to join before, in fact, they are taken into the Union.

On the candidate side, the aspiring country side, I think there is also the need to know that by joining the Union, they will be, in fact, helping their people, their citizens. They will not be joining an economic union in which they cannot compete, in which they cannot afford to contribute. So I think on both sides, there are reasons for the decision to be taken extremely seriously. We, the United States, support very strongly the continued integration of the Western Balkans into the European Union and into NATO for that matter.

Obviously, it is up to the European Union to decide the pace and the process and the rules for how it is going to take place. What we can do in order to assist the process and to the extent possible to facilitate it is to help the candidate countries meet the standards necessary in order to qualify for EU membership. There is a long list of reforms that each country needs to make, both economic, social, and political that in each of the cases of the aspiring countries we are doing our best from our Embassies, from our capitals, to help the country meet the reform requirement.

In many cases, it is an issue of rule of law. The European Union understandably wants to ensure that corruption and organized crime which is, of course, a factor in all of the countries of Europe is something that the new members, the aspiring members are going to be able to effectively address so they don't bring additional problems into the Union when they join.

Mr. MEEKS. Let me ask this question and then I will yield and come back. One of the biggest issues that I think and that is of concern is how the aligning of energy in the region is dealt with and the climate policies with the principles of the EU. And I understand that this is one of the most demanding chapters that the EU and the EU accession, both in cost and legislation that you were talking about needed to be passed. Coal no longer can play such a role in these countries' energy future.

Furthermore, when we see things like Greece is entertaining Russia's plans to solve some of its energy questions, what messages, if any, have we been sending from the U.S. on this front and how can we be sure to kind of integrate the Balkan countries in a new energy system? And how can we reverse this trend and aid the countries in their energy plans so this is lined up so that we can make sure we are working collectively together in that regard?

Mr. YEE. Thank you for that question. I think the European Union, along with the United States and the members, the countries that are aspiring to EU membership, are all very much focused on the need to align energy strategies, national strategies in a way that makes each country as diversified as possible, as energy independent as possible and as efficient as possible in its use of available energy sources.

One of our big emphases now is to help countries in the Western Balkans which are dependent on natural gas from a single source, in this case Russia, also Central Europe the same case, to be less dependent and to diversify the supplies and routes of gas to their countries. This is a particular emphasis now because in recent years, in 2009 and 2006 there have been cases in which natural gas has been cut off in the winter and countries have realized the need to diversify. So this has been identified as a priority by the European Union.

We are working very closely with our European Union partners and the aspiring countries to try to develop pipeline systems that will ensure there is a flow of gas to the countries that are reliant on gas imports, so they are not reliant on one source. They can have more than one pipeline supply.

Also, we are encouraging diversification of energy types, so it is not only gas. It is renewables. It is also domestic, indigenous exploration and exploitation of energy sources. So it is not entirely just one country or one source.

We are also supporting the European Union's efforts to develop a common energy market in which the countries cooperate in how they align their energy strategies so that it is more efficient and they are able to deal with energy exporters, such as Russia, in a way that they are not divided or worked one off the other in a way that is not advantageous to the aspiring countries.

Mr. MEEKS. Ms. Fritz, is there anything you want to add to that?

Ms. FRITZ. Yes, I would like to add the problems of energy supply and energy issues in the region are pretty broad. They include short fall for a generation. They also include aging infrastructure. As DAS Yee mentioned, they rely on Russia for gas supply. They also have low tariffs and high subsidized energy prices, or I am sorry, highly subsidized energy prices and that also continues to hinder capital investment in the sector as well as promote inefficiencies.

USAID is supporting these countries on diversifying their energy supply by supporting infrastructure investments. We, over the last 10 years, have worked with transmission operators within the countries to highlight and outline and identify the most at-risk infrastructure and to bring World Bank and local resources to the tune of $1 billion. So we have improved the connectivity between the countries so that when you have an excess producer like Bosnia or Albania, that they can share, they can trade their energy resources with countries that don't have enough.

We also work heavily in improving energy efficiency. We do that because these systems are highly inefficient. If we can save the amount of energy that they are using, then that not only is it environmentally better, but financially it helps them as well. The example I used in my testimony was an example of Albania where we provided $300,000 worth of technical assistance and advice to help them to reduce losses in their system. They basically reaped $75 million worth of rewards from that effort.

In addition, the World Bank is putting up a loan of $150 million to Albania for energy and USAID has been asked by the Albanian Government to help them to manage those resources in the best way possible. So our assistance is helping to facilitate trade in the region, improve energy efficiency and also to address some of the infrastructure issues in the region.

Mr. MEEKS. Thank you.

Mr. ROHRABACHER. Thank you, Mr. Meeks. So you just mentioned energy efficiency. Is the level of energy production increased in these last 20 years in that region?

Ms. FRITZ. I will have to get back to you on actual figures. I do not know.

Mr. ROHRABACHER. You know about efficiency, but you don't know if there is more energy available for the region?

Ms. FRITZ. I do know that the needs will grow as the economies do grow in the region and I can get back to you on that.

Mr. ROHRABACHER. The economies are growing in the region?

Ms. FRITZ. Yes, they are.

Mr. ROHRABACHER. What is the growth rate for these countries?

Ms. FRITZ. They have slowed. After 2008, the economy slowed and in some cases reversed.

Mr. ROHRABACHER. No, but I mean do you have a growth rate like they have grown at an average of 2 percent a year, 3 percent a year or something like that?

Mr. YEE. Overall, in the Balkans, the growth rate has been about 10 percent since 1990.

Mr. ROHRABACHER. 10 percent since 1990, so that is ½ percent per year, is that what you are talking about?

Mr. YEE. It has been very slow.

Mr. ROHRABACHER. So that is not really good growth at all, is it? That, in fact, would be considered pretty much stagnation, wouldn't it?

Ms. FRITZ. Well, for countries coming out of war, I think it is understandable.

Mr. ROHRABACHER. In fact, it is just the opposite, is it not, when someone is coming out of a conflict that is when they have the highest rate of growth as compared to later on once their economy has been solidified? I think your calculus is wrong there.

Let me ask you this about—so it doesn't appear that there has been much economic progress because everybody seems to be looking about being in the EU and that is going to be the big solution and we know Croatia has at least become part of the EU.

What is it that they have to do? What are some of the requirements for all these other countries that the EU is making demands that they do this, this, and this? Could you give me three of the demands that are being made of these struggling countries?

Mr. YEE. Well, thank you for the question, Mr. Chairman. The answer is that for each of the countries it is slightly a different case on what they need to do. One of the main things that each country needs to be able to do is to make the economy competitive with other members of the European Union. So it is spending levels with respect to GDP. It is ability to meet expenses, state expenses, maintain a budget in other words. It is ability to collect taxes, pay pensions, basic things that any economy in the world would need to do, it needs to be done in a certain level.

Mr. ROHRABACHER. So before they can become part of the EU, demands that are being made are that they have to set up a system that is approved by the EU in terms of their tax collection would you say?

Mr. YEE. It has to meet the EU standards, Mr. Chairman. So across the board in economic criteria of what is needed in order to have a healthy economy within the European Union, the EU has certain standards.

Mr. ROHRABACHER. So it has been 20 years and you are just talking about structural changes that what you are suggesting now are sort of what could be made by democratic government. They could say we are going to collect our taxes in a different way, etcetera. So what is the hold up?

Mr. YEE. Well, the economy, of course, Mr. Chairman, is one big factor. There is also the judiciary. There is the public administration. There is the rule of law overall that needs to be met, the ability to fight corruption and organized crime, the ability of a government to meet its defense and security needs, basically to fit in with the rest of the other 28 members. And as we have seen in the case with Croatia, it was able to meet the standards with difficulty, of course, with numerous reforms, changes including to its constitution. Croatia was able to meet those demands.

Montenegro is also making progress. They have opened, I believe, about 18 negotiating chapters with the European Union, so they are moving ahead. It is a slow and difficult process, but countries have shown that with the right political will, with the right economic conditions, discipline, they are able to make progress on that track.

Mr. ROHRABACHER. Making progress means nothing then unless they are part of the EU. I mean I hear this making progress, I mean I managed to get up and get out of bed today. It seems to me what we have is a total stagnation for 20 years in the largest part of what was a conflict situation.

And Ms. Fritz, I am sorry, that after wars is when economies grow at their fastest rate actually. And it is when you are rebuilding your economy that you have growth. That is by definition, but we haven't had that growth. And it seems to me what we are doing today is we are not celebrating the Dayton Accords. We are marking the fact that they happened 20 years ago.

And it didn't sound like, to me, that you were telling me that we are actually making progress toward taking care of parts into the corruption issue. So the corruption issue is one of the issues keeping these countries out of the EU. Is that correct?

Mr. YEE. That is correct, Mr. Chairman. The ability to fight corruption, organized crime, other serious criminal issues is an important factor being weighed by the European Union as it considers members.

Could I also add, Mr. Chairman, that I would agree with you completely that the progress in Western Balkans has not been as fast and as far as we would like and I think the countries of the region themselves would agree that the European Union would agree. However, as you mentioned yourself, Mr. Chairman, in your opening remarks, there has been progress. Croatia has joined the European Union and the NATO alliance.

Mr. ROHRABACHER. We can keep talking about Croatia, but let us talk about, for example, Serbia. Would you say that they continue to have high level corruption problems in Serbia?

Mr. YEE. Serbia, Mr. Chairman, is actually, I think, a bright spot on the Western Balkan map. In terms of its accession to the European Union, they have reached an agreement brokered by the European Union with Kosovo on normalization of relations. This has allowed them to become a candidate—to open accession negotiations with the European Union, so they are moving ahead.

Mr. ROHRABACHER. I think the question was about corruption.

Mr. YEE. Fighting corruption is one of the challenges that they as well as the other Western Balkans countries face. It certainly is an issue of concern. It is one of the areas in which——

Mr. ROHRABACHER. So give me a reading there for Serbia, the Serbian Government in terms of their effort to eliminate corruption. Sounds like you are giving them an A, but when I am listening, I am trying to figure out if that is an A or——

Mr. YEE. Mr. Chairman, I wouldn't want to assign a rating, but there are international organizations, Transparency International, World Economic Reform.

Mr. ROHRABACHER. Is there any indication that there are politically-motivated persecutions going on and prosecutions going on in Serbia today?

Mr. YEE. Politically-motivated prosecutions?

Mr. ROHRABACHER. Prosecutions, yes.

Mr. YEE. None come to mind, Mr. Chairman.

Mr. ROHRABACHER. You are not aware of any politically-motivated prosecutions, all right.

Let me just, well, we will go through a second round, but Mr. Sires, you may proceed.

Mr. SIRES. Thank you, Mr. Chairman. Can you tell me what the level of influence, Russia's influence is in the Western Balkans today, the Russian influence?

Mr. YEE. Thank you for that question, Mr. Sires. Russia, like many other countries in Europe, is interested in increasing its influence and its business interests in the Western Balkans. We have seen an increase in Russian interest in the Western Balkans through finance, banking, through energy, where it has been present for some time. I think I want to start by saying that Russia has played a positive role in the Western Balkans in such instances, in such countries as Bosnia and Herzegovina, where Russia is a member of the Peace Implementation Council for Bosnia and Herzegovina. We have worked successfully with Russia at advancing shared interests in the Balkans which are including stability and security of the region.

We, of course, are watchful of what Russia is up to the Balkans, particularly in light of what has happened Ukraine. We listen very carefully, follow very closely what Russian diplomats are saying. We noticed of late in last September, last fall, Mr. Lavrov made a statement saying that Russia considers NATO enlargement or NATO accession of Western Balkans to be a provocative act. We, of course, disagree with that. We don't believe NATO is directed at any country. It is a defensive alliance. It is a positive factor of stability in the Western Balkans. So I point that out as an area which we disagree, but we are still able to work with Russia. I think it is important that we remain vigilant as to what they are actually doing, both in terms of their business and their political actions in the Western Balkans.

Mr. SIRES. Are they nervous at all on what has happened with the Ukraine? Are the Balkans nervous at all after seeing what happened in Crimea and Ukraine?

Mr. YEE. I think, Mr. Representative, it is fair to say that many countries in Europe, including the Western Balkans, have watched what Russia has done in Ukraine with great consternation and concern about, first of all, the stability, security of Europe, the strength and integrity of the European order of principles on which——

Mr. SIRES. But, you know, it struck me that you said the Russians have been helping these countries, and you have been working with the Russians, so which is it? I mean——

Mr. YEE. Mr. Representative, it is both. Russia in some occasions, in some instances is a partner with which we work not only in the Western Balkans. As you know, Mr. Representative, we work with Russia in fighting, countering violent extremism, counterterrorism, on the Iran nuclear negotiations.

In Ukraine, we clearly have a different position. We have been urging our European partners and working with our Europeans to insist that Russia abide by its agreements that it signed.

Mr. SIRES. Ms. Fritz, do you have anything to add to this? Can you add something to this?

Ms. FRITZ. USAID is not engaged on countering Russian pressure or aggression in any way. We are a development agency, so no, sir.

Mr. SIRES. You don't want to say anything. Can you tell me what progress has been made since Serbia and Kosovo signed the agreement of principles governing the normalization of relations in 2013?

Mr. YEE. On what basis?

Mr. SIRES. Any progress that they have made. I mean, obviously——

Mr. YEE. Yes, Representative Sires, thanks very much. That is actually another area where we feel there has been some progress made in the Western Balkans. That is the agreement between Kosovo and Serbia to normalize the relations in accordance with an agreement brokered by the European Union in April 2013.

The progress in implementing that agreement has been slow, but it has been steady. We have seen even in February where the two sides, both countries met to work out an agreement on the integration of the judicial system throughout Kosovo for all Kosovo citizens, there are now agreements being worked out on other basic issues affecting citizens lives, telecoms, energy. Eventually, there will be——

Mr. SIRES. Do you feel that in 2015, they remain fully committed to this?

Mr. YEE. Yes, absolutely, Mr. Sires. Both sides have been negotiating in good faith. Both sides see their futures linked to this process of normalization in order to gain what they both want which is to be integrated with the European Union.

Mr. SIRES. Thank you very much, Mr. Chairman.

Mr. ROHRABACHER. We will have a short second round. Mr. Meeks, go right ahead.

Mr. MEEKS. Let me ask Ms. Fritz. How has the USAID programs in the Western Balkans helped to build tolerance between communities? And how much work remains to be done to heal some of the scars of the 1990s? Because to me, we want to make sure that we don't ever go back there and the question of the different ethnic groups. And what I hope our work is is to help build that kind of tolerance so that we can have a more prosperous future.

Ms. FRITZ. Thank you for that question, Mr. Meeks. We have continuing programs on ethnic reconciliation in all four of the former Yugoslav republics in which we are working. So, for example, in Bosnia, we have a variety of activities. We work in the schools to promote ethnic tolerance. We are working with 15 pairs of communities that were divided during the war to promote ethnic reconciliation between those communities. We worked with youth on building ethnic tolerance through sports.

In Kosovo, our effort has been a little bit different. We have focused on helping to establish the ethnically Serb majority municipalities that came out of the Ahtisaari Plan and helping Kosovo Albanians and Kosovo Serbs to work together in building those institutions.

In Macedonia, our focus has been totally related to the schools. Schools in Macedonia are mostly mono-ethnic, meaning that ethnic Macedonian children are in one school, ethnic Albanian kids are in another. So our efforts have been connecting over 260 mono-ethnic schools with one another so that kids have a chance to know kids from other ethnicities. We partnered with the Department of Defense on that project where we have renovated over 40 schools and have worked also with the Macedonian Government which has put up almost $800,000 to also renovate the schools. And local communities, local municipalities have also put up on average 30 percent toward the cost of those projects. This effort has impacted more than 20,000 kids in Macedonia.

And then in Serbia, our efforts have been a little bit different. We focus on economic development in the southern part of Serbia, so in south Serbia where ethnic Albanians live, and in Sanjak where ethnic Bosniaks live, to build economic development and build ties between the central government and these disadvantaged regions. So we have different approaches in each country. It remains front and center of our concerns and our programming because of the scars from the war.

Mr. ROHRABACHER. There has been a vote called, and so I will have a couple of minutes for my second round of questions and then we will be in recess until the end of the next vote that we have or whatever that vote is.

Let me ask, I guess we are opposing, Mr. Yee, the Serbian request for a referendum that they might become, leave their part of the government with Bosnia, is that right? And we are opposing that?

Mr. YEE. Mr. Chairman, thank you for the question. I believe you are referring to the Republic of Srpska's announcement or one party within the Republic of Srpska announced over the weekend in its party congress that if its goals for a greater autonomy were not met by, I believe, 2018, it would want to move toward independence.

Mr. ROHRABACHER. Right.

Mr. YEE. So I think as a general principle, Mr. Chairman, our view is that we need, the United States, needs to continue to support wholeheartedly the sovereignty and territorial integrity of Bosnia and Herzegovina, that there is, in fact, a reform process underway that is led by the European Union and the United States, that is designed to address the desire of the people, not only the Republic of Srpska, but of the federation of the whole country in getting adequate——

Mr. ROHRABACHER. Got it. Well, let me note that it doesn't seem to me we backed the Kosovars right, so determination. And the Serbs certainly didn't like that. And now when you have some Serbs who don't want to—who want their right of self-determination, we just seem to have a double standard. And I think that double standard is quite demonstrable over these last 20 years.

Now what we have is then from what I am getting, I keep hearing the word progress, but it seems to me that what we have got is stagnation and when you have 1½ or just ½ percentage economic growth a year over a 20-year period what you have are people living in desperation because that growth generally would not impact on some of the people who are struggling there to earn a living and live decent lives. But instead, quite often that type of growth pattern services an elite and or is syphoned off into the government in some way.

So I am from the—I know we can use the word progress over and over again. I don't get that from your testimony. I will just have to say that right off the bat and I think if things are not acceptable, if the status quo is not acceptable, it is only giving us this very low growth rate. And I might add people who are on hold to get into the EU for all of these years, it seems that some decisions need to be made to change the situation, not simply to stay on hold until accession into the EU will solve all of these problems.

This hearing is now in recess and the next panel will come up as soon as we get back with this vote. Thank you.

[Recess.]

Mr. ROHRABACHER. This hearing will come to order. I wonder if someone could close that door.

Mr. DIOGUARDI. The reason why they opened it was it got so warm, but now that a lot of people have left, maybe it is better. Just close one side. All right, close them both. The State Department has left, so it is nice and cool now.

Mr. ROHRABACHER. All right. For our next panel we have Ivan Vejvoda, senior vice president of programs, German Marshall Fund here in Washington, DC, from 2010 to 2013, he was the executive director of the Balkan Trust for Democracy Program. And before that, he was the advisor to the Serbian Government and a long-time advocate for democracy in the region.

Next we have Joseph DioGuardi.

Mr. DIOGUARDI. ''DioGuardi,'' in Italian, means God protects.

Mr. ROHRABACHER. A former Member of Congress, and a prominent Albanian-American leader. He worked to focus the attention of the American Government on the Balkans. He is responsible for helping to bring about the first congressional hearing on Kosovo that we ever had. That goes all the way back to 1987 and today he is president of the Albanian American Civic League and is very active in the region. So we are very pleased to have both of you with us today. I would ask you to take 5 minutes and then we will go into questions from there. First, Mr. Vejvoda.

STATEMENT OF MR. IVAN VEJVODA, SENIOR VICE PRESIDENT, PROGRAMS, GERMAN MARSHALL FUND OF THE UNITED STATES

Mr. VEJVODA. Mr. Chairman, thank you very much for your kind introduction and thank you again for organizing this hearing. As you said, there hasn't been one in 2 years and I would submit to you that that is already a sign of progress. That means that there hasn't been anything radical in the region that would provoke a hearing. And I would like to try and say why I believe there has been progress over all these years and it is an honor to be testifying with the Honorable DioGuardi. Thank you so much.

This is about the integration post Second World War Europe, a part of Europe that was left behind the Iron Curtain. Of course, the former Yugoslavia was not. It was in between NATO and the Warsaw Pact, a relatively independent country in terms of its foreign policy. And it slumbered into complete destruction when everybody thought there would never be war in Europe at the end of the 20th century. My country disappeared in front of me and is today seven countries.

Why has there been progress? Well, very simply because there has been serious reconciliation. We haven't talked at all about regional cooperation which is very intense. Just to give you two examples, the military intelligences of all the countries regularly meet twice a year to exchange experiences, youth meets, cultural festivals. There has been a reconstitution of the cultural and societal space after a conflict rather rapidly. We like to say in the region, I am from Belgrade myself, that wars are quick to happen, but they also subside very quickly and people get back to their business.

In spite of all the difficulties that remain, I need not remind you and this country that the scars of the Civil War remain after a long time, after that conflict as we celebrate 150 years of the end of the War. I think here we have moved very rapidly. And the fact that we have a European Union that is, in essence, a peace project after World War II and having to impede war is the main reason why these countries want to join, because they were not democratic. They were not encompassed by this peace project and the fact that the European Union has been so long as peace is one of the key reasons why they want to join. Nobody in the region is oblivious to the fact that Europe has problems, that the Euro zone is in crisis, that growth rates are slow.

And let me just give you one financial statistic. Greece, at the height of the crisis in 2010, had a GDP of $300 billion. If you put all the GDPs of all the former six Yugoslav republics, it barely reached $200 billion. What I am saying is these are small countries. They are weak economies. They had growth rates up until Lehman Brothers disappeared off the streets of New York of 7 to 8 percent. And thus, we suffered with the rest of the world back to low growth rates of 1 to 2 percent, minus 1 percent. And I would say there is nothing unusual in the Balkans about that because that is what happened to the rest of the world.

These countries are highly dependent on foreign direct investments. If you look at the trade patterns, we are fully trading with the European Union and the United States. We have many companies from the U.S. in the region. And in fact, they were calling from the Senate, Chris Murphy visited the region recently and was able to see for himself.

In comparison, Russia is very low on all of those charts in terms of aid and public forums and we can get back to that if you wish.

So what I am saying is that the European Union has put in a lot of money. USAID has been a key actor as has been the U.S. Government. Only yesterday, the German Foreign Minister

Steinmeier visited Belgrade to see how things were progressing. He gave high marks for the reforms in Serbia and of course, complimented both Kosovo and Serbia on the advance they were making. These are historical, difficult challenges. And the fact that the leaders of both Kosovo and Serbia have found it in themselves to make this historical compromise and to move forward with all the difficulties, I would submit to you that it is great progress.

Of course, the fact that the growth rates are low that we have very high youth unemployment. In Bosnia, youth unemployment is above 60 percent. And the fact that we have a brain drain again is not unusual. Look at Spain. Look at Italy. Look at Portugal. Lots of young professionals, IT, are moving north into Scandinavia and into Germany. Again, I want to relativize the fact that we have problems because those of us around us have problems.

But I would like to underscore that it is about politics and geopolitics here. This region is what I call the inner courtyard of Europe. We are surrounded in the Western Balkans by full EU, full NATO member states. And all of the governments for the past 15 years, I take the fall of Milosevic as kind of the last hurdle, as the region moves forward, have determined to both join the EU and to join NATO except Serbia that still seeks a situation of neutrality. And the fact that there is this determination in spite of all is very important. And thus, I think, an invitation coming to Montenegro to join NATO, of course, if the marks are high in the boxes that it has to tick off, is most welcome because it demonstrates that the open-door policy of NATO is the reality. After 2009, so it is 6 years since the last enlargement round of NATO, and taking in Montenegro which would make the full northern coast of the Mediterranean, that is the only little part that remains not part of NATO would be symbolically and geopolitically very important.

And so the EU is working very hard and I would like to underscore the role of Germany. Along with other EU member states, it has taken a lead role. Chancellor Merkel has convened something called the Berlin Process. All the prime ministers of the region were convened to Berlin. They will meet again in Vienna in August and they were in Brussels just 10 days ago with the High Representative Mogherini to look at concrete infrastructure projects. Serbia and Kosovo are negotiating a highway that they will build together. A railroad is being built, a high-speed one between Belgrade and Budapest. So in spite of these difficulties and no one wants to underestimate them or neglect them, that is what life is about, to confront the challenges. I would say that there is leadership.

And I would also like to underscore the importance of civil society and the strength that it has and it requires full support from donors like USA, from the Balkan Trust that is still active. And thus this combination of leadership with support from the United States and the European Union, I think, will help us achieve that Europe whole, free, and at peace that is, I think, a common goal to all of us.

Thank you, Mr. Chairman.

[The prepared statement of Mr. Vejvoda follows:]

United States Congress

House of Representatives

Committee on Foreign Affairs

Subcommittee on Europe, Eurasia and Emerging Threats

Hearing:

Progress and Challenges in the Western Balkans

April 29, 2015

Washington D.C.

TESTIMONY

IVAN VEJVODA

Senior Vice President / Programs

The German Marshall Fund of the United States

Mr. Chairman, thank you for the invitation to come and testify before you today at this important juncture in the path of the Western Balkans toward further peace and stability as they continue their integration in the euro-Atlantic community. It is an honor to be here before this Subcommittee of the House of Representatives of the U.S. Congress. I am here to offer my personal views on the current issues regarding the region as well as to assess the progress made and challenges that the Western Balkans are confronting.

Introduction: The Western Balkans in a changing world.

In a world gripped by many a crisis and conflict zone, still grappling with a return to more sustained patterns of economic growth, the Western Balkans seem, all things being equal, an oasis of peace. A violent conflict at the end of the 20th Century wiped off the map of Europe a country called Yugoslavia and in its stead brought about the formation of 7 countries (one of which is not recognized by a number of countries). It is twenty years since the Dayton Peace Accords were achieved at the Wright-Patterson Air-force base in Ohio in November 1995 and then signed in Paris in December of that year ending the war in Bosnia and Herzegovina. A NATO bombing campaign in 1999 lasting 78 days and targeting what was then the Federal Republic of Yugoslavia (Serbia including Kosovo and Montenegro), led to the departure of a Serbian state administration from Kosovo which in turn led to Kosovo's unilateral declaration of independence in February 2008 (to date recognized by 110 member states of the United Nations, and 23 of the 28 European Union member states). A brief conflict in Macedonia (country that had otherwise managed to peacefully separate itself from former Yugoslavia) in 2001 ended with a framework Ohrid Agreement signed by the conflicting parties leading to peace.

An oasis of peace because notwithstanding all the existing challenges in further consolidating peace, security and stability, strengthening democratic institutions and the rule of law, all the countries and governments of the region are dedicated and determined to join both the European Union (EU) and NATO (with the exception of Serbia for NATO).

Both the EU and NATO thus continue to have key roles for the present and future of the Western Balkans in their own specific ways.

The European Union

The political peace project that is the EU has been a fundamental inspiration and guiding light for the region. The Western Balkans are part of core geographical Europe. They are completely surrounded by EU and NATO member states to their North, East, South and West. They are the "inner courtyard" of Europe. We are not talking here about "neighborhood", or the "marches" of Europe, but countries and a joint population of about 16 million people that all wish to join the EU, and whose history, culture, economy and society are inextricably linked with that of Europe.

The EU's summit in June 2003 in Thessaloniki under the then Greek Presidency was a crucial moment in that it opened the road for the accession to full membership in the EU when they met all the relevant Copenhagen Criteria (defined by the EU in 1993).

The conflict and disappearance of Yugoslavia from the map of post-World War II Europe was a reminder of the fact that history could repeat itself in the darkest of ways. Thus the example of the process of reconciliation and post-war reconstruction of Europe through building institutions that would foster cooperation, stability and peace, and so avoiding Europe's troubled and violent two century history – has been an inspiration and roadmap for the region of the Western Balkans.

In particular the post-war Franco-German reconciliation and all that it entailed has been followed and replicated in multiple dimensions.

The existence and historical success of the European Union in establishing a protracted period of peace and stability is the key reason why the region of the Western Balkans is an oasis of peace today. The EU is the main source of inspiration for reform and specific democratic and economic policies in the Western Balkan countries so as to better their lot, improve their democratic institutions and procedures and painstakingly overcome the deep-seated legacies of their authoritarian past.

The conditionality set forth by the EU's accession provides stringent, rigorous guidelines that lead the countries through their democratic institutional reform processes, in particular in strengthening the rule of law, the judicial system, the division of powers, and the upholding liberal democratic values. The enshrining and securing of the basic freedoms and the empowering of citizens to seek a deepening of democratic legitimacy in a world in which the disillusionment with and even cynicism about government, democratic representation are hallmarks of many a society confronted with major economic challenges – are fundamental European values.

The citizens of the region of the Western Balkans as well as their elected administrations are of course not oblivious to the crisis and inward-turning of the EU and its member states. What is termed the "renationalization" of policies, countries going back on the commitment of sharing sovereignty, demanding more say in their own affairs, leading to a questioning of the democratic legitimacy of the European Commission, European Parliament and the European Council, are visible and palpable. The crisis in the Eurozone (in spite of the fact that countries such as Slovenia, Slovakia, Estonia, Latvia, Lithuania have joined, and some very recently) is also being followed carefully.

What is also heard and seen is the so-called "fatigue" with enlargement. Jean-Claude Juncker President of the EU Commission, famously said at the beginning of his tenure that in these next five years there would be no new enlargement. It was not even necessary to state that since no country was going to be ready in the next five years. The earliest any of the countries that are negotiating entry (Montenegro, Serbia, and then Albania, Macedonia, Bosnia and Herzegovina and Kosovo at different stages in the process) can at earliest be ready toward the end of this decade.

What is much more significant is that even as the EU "muddles through" this crisis of governance and its Eurozone, it formally and in practice continues the process of enlargement. The former EU Commissioner for Enlargement has been renamed EU Commissioner for the Neighborhood and for Enlargement Negotiations (currently Johannes Hahn). And the process moves forward, the assembly line continues in both the administration in Brussels and equally in the aspiring candidate countries.

But notwithstanding the current tumults in the EU, visible clearly o everyone as well as the efforts to overcome them, the countries of the region are determined, committed to pursue their movement towards full EU membership. And as in previous rounds of enlargement (dubbed the most successful policy of the EU in historical terms), this process is of most significant help and support to the democratization and modernization, and thus to the institutional europeanization of these countries.

The EU is at the forefront of responsibility for the process of enlargement. The United States has rightly accepted that the EU take the lead while being present to fully support and in any way be helpful to the process of enlargement and the reform process. The primary responsibility of reform and European and NATO integration resides with the countries themselves. Theirs is the fundamental effort. It behooves them to do the hard work of changing, reforming, democratizing and modernizing their societies.

But it is equally about the credibility of the EU. If the EU is capable of absorbing within its 28 members states and 500 million people another 16 million and ultimately and in time (when all the requirements for membership have been fulfilled) the remaining countries negotiating entry, the EU will prove itself credible of dealing with other issues further afield. This is about core processes in post-1989, post-communist Europe. This is in US parlance "unfinished business". However great the challenges it must be pursued in pro-active manner without relinquishing the conditionalities, but being aware of the geopolitical challenges that are being posed to Europe and the world by the actions of the infringement of the sovereignty of Ukraine by Russia.

The Role of Germany

Germany has within the European Union, as on other matters, taken the lead, but hand in hand with other EU member states, in moving the Western Balkans along the road of full integration. Chancellor Angela Merkel has had a pivotal role in this regard and has systematically reiterated the importance of continuing and supporting the enlargement process to the Western Balkans. She organized a summit of the leaders of the whole region in Berlin in August 2014, inaugurating what is now called the Berlin Process, bringing all the countries together around intensified regional cooperation projects, infrastructure in particular. The next meeting of the Berlin Process will be held in Vienna, Austria in August this year, and next one in Paris in 2016.

This is of the utmost importance because key member states led by Germany have shown how important it is for the EU to show a true spirit of leadership in a key matter that pertains to the origins of the EU, namely the political peace project, but also in showing that even in difficult times the focus on core values that have made the EU what it is today are not discarded.

In that spirit EU leaders have intensified their visits to the region. EU High Representative Federica Mogherini was in the region a month ago. The German Foreign Minister Steinmeier was in Belgrade just yesterday 28 April to show support for the ongoing reform process in Serbia and for the continuation and implementation of the Belgrade-Pristina agreement of April 2013 and subsequent agreements. Both German British Foreign Affairs Ministers were in Bosnia and Herzegovina at the beginning of this year.

The German foreign Minister and his British counterpart Philip Hammond in fact, in a spirit of leadership, proposed last November 2014 a new start for Bosnia-and –Herzegovina. A reform initiative to help Bosnia and Herzegovina move forward toward a Stabilization and Association agreement, to overcome the political stagnation and the lack of badly needed reform. The Bosnian EU integration process has been stalled for years owing to the lack of willingness to move the reform process forward. The focus of the German-British proposal is in the area of economic and social policy as well as on good governance and the rule of law.

Belgrade-Pristina: A Historical Step Forward in Reconciliation and Normalization under European Auspices

The April 13, 2013 agreement was a key step forward in deepening the foundations of peace, stability and security in the region. The dialogue was initiated under the previous administration of President Boris Tadic in March 2011. Given that Serbia had fulfilled all the outstanding requirements related to the International Criminal Tribunal on the Former Yugoslavia (notably arresting and extraditing Radovan Karadzic in 2008 and then Ratko Mladic in 2011), the other key issue was to show political determination and willingness, in the spirit of the European peace project, to begin normalization between Belgrade and Pristina, Serbia and Kosovo. The engaged process was continued under the new Serbian Government led by the Serbian Progressive Party that won the elections in 2001 and then again overwhelmingly in March 2013.

Prime Ministers then Ivica Dacic of Serbia and Hashim Thaci of Kosovo with their delegations worked diligently to find the necessary compromises that would lead to the signing of the agreement. A key and crucial role was played the EU's High Representative for Foreign and Security Policy Baroness Catherine Ashton. With a steady hand, with patience and understanding for the difficulty of the challenge she helped with patience the parties become owners the process, and find their own path toward the compromise. This process has been taken over in the new European Commission by Federica Mogherini the new EU High Representative who has held a meeting on February 9 this year where the parties achieved an agreement on the issue of the judiciary.

Much remains to be done and outstanding issues need to be resolved but the process is in engaged in a European reconciliation spirit, where only peaceful means are the way of a stable and peaceful future.

Serbia expects the beginning of its formal negotiations with the EU by the end of this year. Kosovo at the same time will be signing a Stabilization and Association Agreement with the EU in October this year, as announced by the EU's Special Representative to Kosovo Samuel Zbogar.

Democracy, rule of law and the fight against corruption – in times of economic hard times

In all countries of the region keys challenges remain the eradication of systemic forms of corruption. All countries have made significant strides but there is still much to be done.

The unemployment levels especially among youth which are very high in all countries of the region are one of the greatest challenges that the region confronts. The decline in foreign direct investments (FDI) has dealt a hard blow to employment trends. The region does not have the domestic resources to put in motion significant investments. And thus the importance of support from FDI's and contributions through EU funds, and bilateral donors, including the US and in particular USAID are very important. Private donors such as the Open Society Foundation, of the work of the German Marshall Fund, through its project the Balkan Trust for Democracy are still relevant to support also importantly the sustainability of civil societies in the region.

The freedom of speech and its upholding and defence in the early democratic life is fundamental to a society. The well-being, transparency and accountability of democratic institutions relies on an open public space where the common good and the public interest are voiced and defended.

Civic and democratic life depends on a vibrant civil society and efficient and democratic state responsible to its citizens. This is a daily struggle and duty that has been the staple of any democracy that has been worthy of its name.

The Western Balkans and the Role of NATO

NATO continues to play an important role in the stability and peace of the Western Balkans.

NATO troops are still present in Kosovo to the benefit of both Albanian and Serbian communities there. The number of troops of the NATO-led Kosovo Force has been significantly reduced.

NATO also offers strong political support to the Belgrade-Pristina Agreement of 19 April 2013, and KFOR stands ready to support its implementation within its current mandate. NATO's presence is thus significant both symbolically and practically as the region consolidates the pillars of stability and peace.

All the countries of the Western Balkans (except for Kosovo) have been or are members of the Partnership for Peace Program (Macedonia since 1995, Bosnia and Herzegovina, Montenegro and Serbia since the Riga NATO Summit in 2006). Albania and Croatia became full members in 2009. Macedonia was supposed to join during that same year but because of the unresolved issue of its name with its southern neighbor Greece and the veto put by Greece to Macedonia's joining, it finds itself in limbo. This is a situation that is not conducive to stability and peace in the country itself nor in the region.

The Secretary General of NATO Jens Stoltenberg just last week in an interview endorsed NATO's "open door" policy — in principle.

"It is, he said, a fundamental right of every sovereign nation to decide its own path, including what kind of security arrangements it wants to be part of... Whether NATO shall continue to enlarge is the question which should only be decided by the applicant countries and the 28 allies."

This is an important reminder at a moment when Montenegro is expecting to be possibly invited to join in December following a decision of the North Atlantic Council. In a strong endorsement of Montenegro joining the German Ambassador in Montenegro said that the country should be invited to join in a statement given in Podgorica on February 4 of this year.

It would be a strong signal to the region as a whole that, six years after the last enlargement (to Albania and Croatia), the reality of the "open door" policy be proven an invitation to the next country in line, Montenegro. Such a decision would further strengthen stability, security and peace in the region.

Energy security and energy supplies.

Energy is a fundamental issue when considering the progress and challenges in the region. The whole issue of a much needed diversification of sources of supply and further strengthening regional and European wide interconnections is of the essence. Many of these countries rely completely or largely on Russian (Gazprom's) gas supply for their energy needs. This is the key element of the region's relationship with Russia. During the 2006 and 2009 cutting of Russian gas supplies through Ukraine the region of the Western Balkans was also victim and has troubles in compensating for the lack of flow of gas.

The recent decision of Russia to scrap the South Stream pipeline project and replace it with a Turkish pipeline to which the other countries of the region including Greece would adhere, has been somewhat of a "wake-up call". Russia and Turkey, though, have yet to reach a deal for that plan. South Stream which was a project, years in the making, of Gazprom and major European energy firms such as Italian ENI, German Wintershall, and French EDF, and which was to pass through EU members states Bulgaria, Hungary and end in Austria and Italy, passing through (not yet EU member) Serbia – raised high hopes of securing a steady supply of gas that did not depend on the Ukrainian route. On April 7 he foreign ministers of Hungary, Serbia, Macedonia, Greece and Turkey in Budapest signed an agreement to participate in the so-called Turkish Stream pipeline, were it to go ahead.

The European Union is forging ahead importantly with the project of a European energy union which should lead to unified and regulated policies regarding energy. South Stream was in part stopped in its steps because the European Union rightly required that the possible future pipeline adhere to rules of competitiveness, of the so-called third energy legislative package for an internal gas and electricity market.

Since the transformation, diversification of energy routes and supplies cannot bear fruit in the short term the countries of the region remain dependent on Russian gas and thus have to negotiate the stability and security of supply with Russian/Gazprom authorities.

Imports of LNG would and could be a way of addressing in the immediate and term the issue of diversification and weaning oneself off a single supplier.

This is an important challenge for the region going forward.

Conclusion

The region has made significant strides and is moving in the right direction. Important challenges remain but as part of a broader Euro-Atlantic integration process they partake in a partnership of purpose which supports them in achieving their goal of a democratic consolidated future where stability and peace are the fundamentals.

The circumstances of the world as it entered the economic crisis in 2008 have slowed down not only the economic growth of these countries, but have posed challenges in achieving a more sustained and rapid reform process overall. Nonetheless, even in these circumstances they have moved toward resolving outstanding issues, often engaging in a multitude of forms of regional cooperation in the field of politics, economy, security , cultural exchanges to mutual benefit.

The support of the United States to these processes has been crucial. The continued engagement of the US administration and of USAID remain crucial to the overall success of the democratic reform process and membership in the EU and NATO for these countries. Thus allowing the accomplishment of the full unification of Europe in peace, and stability.

Mr. ROHRABACHER. Thank you. Joe, you are on.

STATEMENT OF THE HONORABLE JOSEPH J. DIOGUARDI, PRESIDENT, ALBANIAN AMERICAN CIVIC LEAGUE (FORMER MEMBER OF CONGRESS)

Mr. DIOGUARDI. Mr. Chairman, thank you so much for this hearing. I know we have many problems to deal with, the United States of America, around the world. Your questions to the State Department were excellent. As an American, I am embarrassed with the lack of clarity and the lack of substance on the answers you got from the State Department and the USAID.

Now you know me as an advocate for human rights, but you may have forgotten that I am the first certified public accountant ever elected to the U.S. Congress. So let me talk about the numbers, because the numbers you heard don't add up.

When you discover that the State Department thinks that our growth rate is less than 10 percent over a long period and as you rightly pointed out that is ½ percent growth annually. Think about now the Albanian people in Kosovo and Macedonia. They have the highest birthrate in Europe today. Now think about the fact that there is no visa liberalization, so there is no way for the youngest population in Europe to go West. They are forced to go to Turkey. But not where there is some real growth like in Germany. That has to be resolved, number one.

And think about the fact that you have this continuing adversarial relationship between the Serbs and the Albanians, at least at the government level. You heard from the State Department that they see hope and integration and normalization. How can there be normalization when every opportunity Serbia gets it says they will never recognize the independence of Kosovo. How can you have European integration when 5 countries today out of the 28 are not recognizing the independence of Kosovo? I don't think they know who the Albanian people are. They are the most pro-American, most pro-democracy, and the most tolerant people in terms of inter-religious tolerance in perhaps, the world today. They share four religions. There are even synagogues. A recent one was built in Albania. So you have Orthodox Christians, Roman Catholics, Muslims, and Jews. They intermarry. This is not a reality for the rest of Europe. This is what we should be supporting. These are the people that on 9/11, from Kosovo and Macedonia, were crying, walking with candles in the street, while the Serbs, the Greeks, Montenegrins, and Macedonians, ethic Slavic Macedonians that is, were dancing for joy in the streets. I just want to remind you, Mr. Chairman, who our friends are in the Balkans.

You are continuing in the path of great chairmen. We started the first hearing with Congressman Dante Fascell, a Democrat. Then Congressman Gilman. Then Congressmen Hyde and Lantos, and now you. And thank God we have this progression, and that America understands that their best friends in the Balkans are the Albanian people.

Now why is this hearing so important? We want to see Southeast Europe integrated into Europe. But the answers you heard—and your questions were excellent but got very few answers—tell us that unless the United States remains not only present, but active in Southeast Europe, there will be no European integration. There will be something that will happen before that that could create violence again. And I hope not. Nobody wants to see that. The problem is that the Albanian people can only take so much. So let us focus on Kosovo and then a few comments on Macedonia.

We had a Pristina-Belgrade agreement 2 years ago heralded by Catherine Ashton. It is now been almost 2 years. Very little of the 15-point agreement has been implemented. And yet, you heard the State Department say that it is mostly done. It is not. In fact, Serbia has yet to dismantle the parallel structures in the north. Now I understand your philosophy and I love it, about ''self-determination.'' But there is a big difference in the self-determination that the Kosovars wanted and the Serbs want. Kosovars were under a genocidal maniac, Slobodan Milosevic. And a lot of that is continuing today. There is racism by the Slavic Macedonians and Slavic Serbs. There is actual racism against the Albanian people today. As you know, they are not Slavs. They should have never been put in a state called Yugoslavia. That was the biggest mistake that was made after World War I.

So where are we going with this at this point? If the State Department thinks that things are in regular order, when Serbia is refusing to recognize Kosovo, refusing to take away the parallel structures and what not. The other problem the State Department has is that it has been much too involved in decisions that have been made within Kosovo. For instance, there was an election. There was an impasse. People did not want a return of the regime of Hashim Thaci. Many people feel he is corrupt and we can say the same thing about some politicians in Macedonia. But what happened was that our State Department—well, I hope not, but it is probable. But the problem is that we have a State Department now that forced the issue. There was a coalition, an opposition that was trying to regularize things in Kosovo and now we have a return of the political elite just switching chairs. Now Mr. Thaci is the deputy to Isa Mustafa who was rated yesterday with the population of Kosovo at 24 percent popularity, but our State Department engineered that back.

Another thing——

Mr. ROHRABACHER. You have 60 seconds. We are way over already.

Mr. DIOGUARDI. Let us look at Mr. Dell. He forces the creation of a road that is supposed to cost $1 billion to connect Albania and Kosovo. It goes to $2 billion. We need jobs in Kosovo, not a road. That road could have been built by local contractors for half price. And where does he end up? In a senior position in Bechtel, the company he aided to get the job. I would say, Mr. Chairman, that we need the U.S. Inspector General for the State Department to look at that.

Let me just conclude with Macedonia. And by the way, I want to be sure that all my written comments are on the record. And in the case of Kosovo, there is an article that was written by our Balkan affairs advisor, Shirley Cloyes DioGuardi, ''Confronting the Roots of Kosovo's Downward Spiral.'' And I would like to make sure that this article is put on the record.

Mr. ROHRABACHER. It will be submitted and put into the record without objection.

Mr. DIOGUARDI. And on Macedonia, we have another article by Irwin Fouere and he was someone who was the former EU Special Representative in Macedonia from 2005 to 2011. I think he knows what he is talking about. And that article is entitled, ''Gruevski Must Resign and Make Way for a Transition Process in Macedonia.'' That article was dated March 23, 2015, so that it is recent, as is the alleged corruption he talks about in that article——

Mr. ROHRABACHER. The article will be put into the record at this point without objection.

Mr. DIOGUARDI. And let me conclude just on the two points, Kosovo and Macedonia. It is in my written comments here, but I would like to make just one concluding comment here on both.

Regarding Kosovo, if the EU is serious about integration, there must be a much more aggressive approach taken for the recognition of Kosovo by all EU countries including Serbia.

Regarding Macedonia, Albanians need to be treated as an equal partner in a state that does not have an ethnic majority, no majority. You have Bulgarians. You have Slavs. And you have the Albanians. But in that state, when it was formed, the constitution in 1992 was formed as a Macedonian state and that still rankles the Albanians today because they are not treated as equal and that is a big problem. The only other option, Mr. Chairman, is federalization. It was talked about back in the early '90s, but that is what Albanians would need if they didn't get a constitution that treated them as an equal state-forming group. They want federalization that will allow them administrative, social, and financial control over their own destiny as part of a Macedonian federation of ethnic Albanians and Slav Macedonians.

The problem we have got in Macedonia is so simple, it is black and white. Macedonia is an apartheid state in the middle of Europe. The Albanians do not live with the Slavs. They live separately, but unequally, and this is the problem today. And now you have Mr. Gruevski being exposed by his own opposition Slavic leader as one of the most corrupt leaders in Europe and the poor Albanian people are sitting there trying to figure out where we fit in all of this.

Mr. ROHRABACHER. Joe, thank you for your time.

Mr. DIOGUARDI. Thank you so much for this opportunity.

[The prepared statement of Mr. DioGuardi follows:]

Statement of Hon. Joseph H. DioGuardi
President, Albanian American Civic League

House Committee on Foreign Affairs
Subcommittee on Europe, Eurasia, and Emerging Threats

"Progress and Challenges in the Western Balkans"

April 29, 2015

US foreign policy in the Balkans is failing once again. Without a just solution to the adversarial relationship that is still evident between Serbia and Kosova sixteen years after NATO airstrikes against Serbia ended the war, there will be no peace and stability in the Balkans. The future of the integration of Southeast Europe into the European Union is at stake.

Kosova

It has been two years since the Prishtina-Belgrade Agreement was signed by Kosova Prime Minister Hashim Thaci and Serbian Prime Minister Ivica Dacic and this committee held a hearing about it. Then EU High Representative for Foreign Policy, Catherine Ashton, who brokered the agreement and called it historic, expected the implementation to take place within weeks of the signing on April 19, 2013. Instead, little of the 15-point agreement has been implemented. Most important, the de facto partition of northern Kosova by Serbia is still unresolved, and Serbia has yet to dismantle its parallel structures there.

Serbia is still demanding rights that go beyond the Ahtisaari Plan (formally the "Comprehensive Proposal for the Kosovo Status Settlement")—on the basis of which Kosova's parliament declared the independence of Kosova on February 17, 2008, and accepted international supervision. The Ahtisaari Plan, which focuses primarily on the protection of minority rights in Kosova, represented the maximum concession of the 92 percent Kosovar Albanian majority for the resolution of Kosova's final status. Meanwhile, the Albanian majority in Southern Serbia—in Presheva, Medvegje, and Bujanovc—do not have anything like the rights that Kosova's Serbian minority has.

Because of the Ahtisaari Plan and because of Serbia's refusal to recognize Kosova's sovereignty, Kosova is independent in name only. Kosova still does not have a seat at the United Nations or in other international bodies, which has also meant that there is little foreign investment. It is also the only country in the Western Balkans without visa-free travel. This has led to massive unemployment, especially among the young (the rate is 60 percent or more), many of whom are highly educated, but they are without jobs and a path to a future in Kosova. As a result, several thousand have left Kosova for Western Europe since December, most illegally. Many commentators have sighted the loosening of border restrictions via Serbia into Hungary.

But the real reason for the flight is the loss of belief in the West, which, as AACL Balkan Affairs Adviser Shirley Cloyes DioGuardi stated in her December 2014 article "Confronting the Roots of Kosova's Downward Spiral" (that I am submitting for this hearing's Congressional Record), facilitated the return to power of the political elite that "has prevented Kosova from flourishing and prospering for the past decade." Once the six-month stalemate, following Kosova's general elections on June 8, 2014, was brought to an end by the break-up of the coalition that opposed the return of Hashim Thaci as Prime Minister and his ruling Democratic Party of Kosova (PDK), the loss of hope in Kosova has become staggering.

The Albanian political elite in Kosova have been getting richer and richer, while most of the Albanian people have been getting poorer and poorer. The State Department needs to take responsibility for propping up the Thaci government, which has become a racketeering enterprise. The loss of hope among Albanians, the most historically pro-Western, pro-American population in Europe, also is connected with the complicity of the EU and the United States in some of the most flagrant examples of the corruption that plagues Kosova. (One EU operative, a German national was convicted of stealing 4.3 million Euros from Kosova.) It is also time for the Administration to acknowledge the role that its former Ambassador to Kosova, Christopher Dell (2009-2012), played in pushing through a deal for the Bechtel Corporation to build a $1 billion highway from Kosova to Albania (the cost of which rose to $2 billion and that could have been built for far less money by local contractors) and then landing a senior position with Bechtel in Africa upon leaving his post in Kosova. The construction and its exorbitant cost occurred when Kosova was (and still is) a country unable to create jobs and political stability. This is totally unacceptable and should be investigated by the Inspector General of the US State Department.

Macedonia

In Macedonia, the deteriorating political situation and the relationships between ethnic groups—in the one country in the Western Balkans where no ethnicity has a majority—is acute, and yet both the US government and the European Union are failing to address the unfolding crisis. As Erwan Fouere, the former EU Special Representative in Macedonia from 2005 to 2011, has stated in his March 23, 2015, article in *Balkan Insight*, entitled "Gruevski Must Resign and Make Way for Transition Process," which I am submitting for this hearing's Congressional Record, "the extent of the alleged corruption and intimidation perpetrated by the prime minister, Nikola Gruevski, and his ruling party VMRO-DPMNE, has been brought out into the open" through the shocking revelations made available to the public by ethnic Macedonian opposition leader Zoran Zaev about the vast wire-tapping operation conducted by Gruevski. In another an April 2015 article, Fouere concluded that today Macedonia "is a country governed by fear and intimidation with a ruling party, whose ethno-nationalist and populist agenda has created new fault lines in an already fragile environment," the most alarming of which are the reopening of deep tensions between the ethnic Albanian and ethnic Macedonian communities.

Meanwhile, Ali Ahmeti, the leader of the Democratic Union for Integration (DUI), the junior ethnic Albanian party in the ruling coalition, has played the nationalist card when he finds it politically expedient and has remained quiet about the wiretapping scandal, which apparently is the result of his party's involvement in corruption with their senior coalition partner, VMRO-DPMNE, led by Prime Minister Gruevski, now accused publicly by the Macedonian opposition party, the Social Democratic Union of Macedonia, of a massive criminal political and economic agenda, especially against the large Albanian population in Macedonia.

When it comes to Macedonia, the key reality is that the Ohrid Framework Agreement of 2001, which ended the armed conflict that year between ethnic Macedonians and Albanians and put forward a number of constitutional and legal changes designed to overturn a decade of discrimination against Albanians, has yet to be fully implemented.

The frustration and growing despair of the large Albanian population in Macedonia with the corrupt Gruevski government, including the complicit Albanian political parties led by Ali Ahmeti and Menduh Thaci, is a figurative bomb that can go off at any time, especially with an economy that produces only government jobs that go mostly to ethnic Macedonians and then only to those who vote for the corrupt Gruevski/Ahmeti partnership, which is enslaving the whole country politically and economically. Our State Department's Balkan strategy of status quo, which can now be "translated" into Balkan "peace and stability at all costs," has become a daily aspirin or cocktail for the Albanian people to make their pain subside for today while sowing the seeds for Balkan ethnic disintegration, not European integration.

Conclusion

In the end, nothing will be achieved in the Western Balkans without the strong involvement of the United States. The history of the region has shown this to be true. Regarding Kosova, all of the EU Members need to recognize the independence of Kosova and end the country's isolation through economic opportunities. Regarding Macedonia, Albanians need to be treated as an equal partner in a new Constitution of this now failing State, or we must face the option of federalization, which will allow the Albanian people administrative, social, and financial control over their own destiny as part of a Macedonian federation of ethnic Albanians and ethnic Macedonians. Macedonia is already an apartheid State, in which the major ethnic groups live separately, but not equally, and this must be corrected. Otherwise, Macedonia will not survive as a sovereign state that can be integrated into the European Union.

Mr. ROHRABACHER. I will proceed with some questions and then Mr. Meeks will follow and the second swing, we will do that as well.

Let me ask our friend from the German Marshal Fund, has the debt like for these Balkan countries in the last—we have 20 years. Okay, we have got 20 years since the Dayton Accords. We know that they are—and I know you believe that this is just a global trend in terms of an economy that was not producing a great deal of growth. We noticed that there was a World Bank loan of $150 million. How much debt are these countries in now? And what does that mean in terms of their economic viability and in terms of being able to function while paying the interest on the debt?

Mr. VEJVODA. Well, again, nothing special about the Balkans. Like most of the countries in the world, they have a varying level of debt. In Serbia, I know it is 75 percent of GDP to the debt which is around $25 billion, I think. Other countries also, Croatia, Slovenia, I mean EU member states also, not only Bosnia and Macedonia, Kosovo, Albania, and Montenegro.

The IMF has just concluded an agreement with Serbia just I think a month ago to the level of $3 billion to support the reform process and also the structural reforms that are required. Basically, in the case of Serbia——

Mr. ROHRABACHER. So we are asking for structural reform while burdening them with $2 billion of debt?

Mr. VEJVODA. The structural reforms cannot happen without that support because structural reforms mean that you have to close down companies, so-called public enterprises that are working at a loss in Serbia. When you put them all together, there are roughly 300 companies or more that make a loss of $1 billion a year. So what the IMF and the World Bank are saying, you need to close this down, but of course, there are human stories behind that because that means laying off thousands of people who, in an economy without growth, you know, the state will have that burden to carry it and thus the support from the outside——

Mr. ROHRABACHER. Are we bailing out owners of these companies?

Mr. VEJVODA. No. These are all state-owned companies.

Mr. ROHRABACHER. I know. So it is just a state-owned company and there is no business class of people who are receiving the loan?

Mr. VEJVODA. No. These are loans that—of course, there is the privatization in place, not dissimilar to what is being asked of Greece or Ukraine at this moment. Of course, Greece should have done this a long time ago. It has been a member state of the EU for more than 40 years and a member of NATO for more than 60 years. So I think again, in comparison, things are moving. Yes, at a slow pace. And as a citizen of that region, I am also frustrated by it, but as an analyst, as a political scientist in my previous life, I think it is moving.

Mr. ROHRABACHER. We have Greece as a next door neighbor, as an example, and they are a member of EU and NATO. And then we have all of these other Balkan countries who have been waiting 20 years thinking that NATO and EU would be their economic, give them economic deliverance. By the way, when you say this $2 billion loan, who is that repaid to? Who actually gets the money at the end?

Mr. VEJVODA. It has to be, just as Greece is repaying it to the IMF and the World Bank, Serbia will repay this IMF loan of $3 billion to the IMF.

Mr. ROHRABACHER. Is there actually any private banks that end up being paid for by this? Or is this all a government?

Mr. VEJVODA. This is all in IMF loans. These are not private banks.

Mr. ROHRABACHER. This debt isn't, we are not putting these people in debt to some big German bank some place?

Mr. VEJVODA. No, this is not like the case of Greece.

Mr. ROHRABACHER. You know, I am not sure that people can borrow their way into prosperity. And I know that we are saying that getting these loans are predicated on the reforms necessary for closing up unprofitable operations, that it would be better to having the money spent on things that actually are self-sustaining. I understand that is a good point. But it does seem that all the time when people are talking about all the progress that has been made, all we hear about is Croatia and for the rest of these countries, we are talking about fairly large unemployment. Certainly, of course, right next door we have Greece that is a member of the EU and is a member of NATO and they seem to be having big problems as well.

Are you—let me just get this, are you optimistic that these things are going to be overcome? We have had 20 years now and I am sorry, I don't buy our own Government's analysis of this is a progress line. I know that you wanted to suggest that you thought there was progress as well.

Mr. VEJVODA. There is.

Mr. ROHRABACHER. Outside of Croatia, is this figure correct that 60 percent of youth, young people, are unemployed?

Mr. VEJVODA. In Bosnia.

Mr. ROHRABACHER. In Bosnia. Sixty percent? Do you think that might lead to perhaps when we have ethnic differences and especially when you have people, for example, is there any evidence, for example, that you have that perhaps some of the unemployed youth of this region who are Muslims might be engaged in being recruited to participate in radical Islamic terrorism?

Mr. VEJVODA. There are, but in comparison to countries like France or Belgium or Sweden, we have very low numbers in the region throughout. Maybe from each country, 20, 30 people have gone, Bosnia, Serbia, Kosovo, a little more, Macedonia. There are now statistics. In fact, just yesterday, the European Union has decided to give $10 million euros to the region for greater interoperability between the civilian intelligence services so that they can do their job better, but I think they are doing very well.

Let me just add, and this is something that we didn't mention, there has been very intense cooperation between the United States, DEA, and our domestic civilian services on countering serious organized crime, especially cocaine trafficking from Latin America. A lot of these people are in jail and being tried. So I would like to underscore the interdependency, whether it is of the region with Europe or in this case of the United States with the region. There are FBI offices, I think, in all of these countries and there is very intense work together. So we are not an island separated from the rest of the world. So we share both the travails and the problems.

And I would like simply to make a distinction, Mr. Chairman, if you will allow, between political progress and economic troubles that the rest of the world is seeing. I would say that there has been huge political progress. We were communist countries. There was no freedom of speech, no freedom of association, no human rights. We have made huge strides. You heard from Deputy Assistant Secretary Hoyt Yee that Albania was now given a clean bill of justice on their last elections. It was the last country that didn't have elections that were considered free and fair. The rest of us in the region have that. We go home at 10 in the evening and we know that the votes are well counted. There is, of course, now this allegation of fraud in the case of Macedonia that is being investigated. You heard about that. But I think that citizens now do have the possibility of——

Mr. ROHRABACHER. So you don't really take these charges of corruption and ballot stuffing and——

Mr. VEJVODA. That is what is being investigated, these wire taps and we will see what the prosecution in Macedonia comes up with up. They are very serious allegations. I do not——

Mr. ROHRABACHER. So if we are only going to focus on the political progress, because the economic progress has been so low, we end up having to close our eyes to the other things?

Mr. VEJVODA. No, not at all, not closing our eyes at all. I think, again, the journalists, the citizens, there are strikes in our countries. People stand up for themselves and when they see unemployment or difficulties in government in going about the reforms, people are very supportive of these reforms. In fact, they are more supportive of reforms than joining the EU or NATO because they know it is about us.

So when we talk about the EU and NATO, what has been very clear and we talk about 15 years again in countries like Serbia because it is the fall of Milosevic that really marks the turning point for the region, when that authoritarian ruler was beat by us citizens at the polling station in a free election which we defended in the street, half a million of us went down into the street on October 5, 2000 to defend our freedom.

The case is that people know that freedom is valuable and they defend it, but we again are not an island in the Pacific that lives off coconuts. We are dependent on the world markets. For example, in Serbia we have a huge car plant that is owned by Chrysler-Fiat that has been doing well, but not everyone has the fortune to work in that car factory. So it is about foreign-direct investments. There is no economic domestic capacity in any of our countries. They are not billionaires. They are not Bill Gates or Warren Buffets who can invest. We need to await support either from international financial institutions and I would add the European Bank for Reconstruction and Development and the European Investment Bank.

Mr. ROHRABACHER. I would have to suggest that if the economic situation does not improve and it continues to be more like Greece than like other countries in the world, I predict that the democratic institutions you are talking about will come under even greater pressure and we have to understand that if young people can't find jobs, do end up getting recruited, and if they see that their own Government has certain levels of corruptions, it tends to destabilize the whole country.

Mr. VEJVODA. Mr. Chairman, if I could just add one sentence.

Mr. ROHRABACHER. Yes, sir.

Mr. VEJVODA. To put it all to bluntly, we have done war and we have been there in the '90s. And we have learned what the cost of conflict is. And that is why progress is a fact in this region. Nobody wants to go back there, not the Bosnians, not the Albanians, not the Serbs, because it has been a huge cost to their lives. We have lost 10 years. I had to change my career. I suffered also with my family and others as has everyone in the region and that is why we want to join the European Union and most countries want to join NATO.

Mr. ROHRABACHER. I think you are right and——

Mr. VEJVODA. And so in spite of the resilience, the resilience is important to understand why we want, but of course, there will be examples of young going to fight for the Islamic states.

Mr. ROHRABACHER. Only if they are chronically unemployed and they have no hope in their life. I would certainly agree with your assessment that when people have been through the kind of war, and we have a situation now maybe I should ask you about it. There is a group, there were actually three brothers that were murdered by the Serbians and we were told that there would be some kind of action taken to bring justice to that case. Is there justice being brought to that case, for example?

Mr. VEJVODA. Yes, this is a well-known case. The Bitici brothers and their brother who fortunately is alive met the Serbian prime minister who promised him a face-to-face, that this would be dealt with.

Mr. ROHRABACHER. Has that been dealt with?

Mr. VEJVODA. It has not yet been dealt with, but the prosecution is working full steam on this. I think the Serbian prime minister will be visiting Washington soon at the invitation of Vice President Biden.

Mr. ROHRABACHER. The prosecutor is working full steam and how long has it been?

Mr. VEJVODA. It has been long. It has been long.

Mr. ROHRABACHER. If that is full steam, I wonder what slow pace, if that is full steam. They are not working full steam on it. And there is a lot of things that need to be done full steam and they are not doing it.

Mr. VEJVODA. And unfortunately, it is not only the case with this, but there are journalists who were assassinated under Milosevic's time whose cases are not closed yet also. So it is not only——

Mr. ROHRABACHER. Right. Well, let me put it this way. I think that we have to—we are marking the 20th anniversary. I think if progress continues at the rate that it has been within the next 20 years, you are going to see a disintegration rather than anywhere—anybody could be optimistic about it. Because the political reform—it is not reform, it is political realization of people don't want to kill each other. That will dissipate with time if you have people who are living hopeless lives in these various countries.

And I do not—look, if the EU will loan them, I guess it is not the EU loaning $2 billion, but sitting right next to the EU and the EU has all of these hoops that these countries have got to jump through before they can benefit like the rest of the Europeans and they have been waiting for 20 years and they are still not in the EU. I mean Croatia is the one country that has made it. None of this gives me reason for optimism or especially to use the word progress.

Mr. Meeks, you may go right ahead.

Mr. MEEKS. Thank you, Mr. Chairman. And I think what we may have here is between the chairman and I a classic case of is the glass half full or is the glass half empty. And from what I hear from the chair he says it is half empty. I think I side that it is half full.

Mr. ROHRABACHER. Is there vodka in the glass?

Mr. MEEKS. Not for me. So for me, 20 years is not a long time. And 20 years where we are starting to see that integration is substantial. And I think of—I can't help to come to these—my thinking and to my positions without also looking at a nation that has been here for over 238 years, the United States of America. And I don't see how we can be critical of countries that are trying to get together and work and have the integration in 20 years when we really haven't—still, we are striving to be a more perfect union.

I mean I couldn't help but think about what has taken place just a few short miles from here today, yesterday, in Baltimore where you have got a group of young men, unemployed, no sense of hope, none of those things exist. This is in the United States of America. When I think about the number of individuals who are being recruited from al Qaeda or for ISIS or whatever, right here from the United States of America. So I don't see how I can be so critical of others who are trying to strive and prove themselves just 20 short years when the United States has been trying to do it for over 238 years. It is a fact that the globe is now much smaller than it has been. And we do need to figure out how we integrate it and work collectively together and that is why in my estimation it is important for us and the United States and for the EU to work with other nations who are also striving to be better. There are ethnic differences, so that is why I asked the question before about that, just as there are ethnic differences still in the United States of America. But the only way that we can work that out is to try to figure out how we can talk and work that out and do it collectively as a human community and as a world community.

So I would like to think that the progress that I have seen over the last 20 years where we have come from the slaughtering of human beings on a massive level to where now we are really starting to talk about the corruption that may be there, fixing the economy, fixing this and fixing that, on figuring how we work together better as opposed to how we destroy one another, to me that is truly a glass that is half full.

Now we have still got a long way to go. We have still got to make sure that we would like the full glass and that is what I think that I am hearing some. And Mr. Vejvoda, I am hearing you say that what we are striving to do is to get better. And the economy, Lord knows, we just came out of the greatest recession since the Great Depression here in the United States. And everybody in the EU economy has been suffering when I look at the unemployment rates as going up.

So it is important to me that we have this hearing and we have this kind of dialogue on both ways though because by doing that then maybe we can realize and try to figure out how we can improve and have a better situation.

Now I get concerned because all areas of the world are important and oftentimes when I travel some say well the United States being the world's largest economy is focused here and not there. And that is why I think this hearing is important because the Balkans has to be still on the United States' place as we tend to look at some other places whether it is dealing in Ukraine or dealing in Asia or dealing in some other part, we have to make sure the Balkans is still in our focus because it is such still a key part of the world. And until we can do that—so I get concerned, for example, in the U.S. budget as I look as we put a lot of dollars now toward the Ukraine situation. I look that the focus is less on what is taking place in the Balkans. And so I am wondering how we make up for the lower levels of funding that remain so that we can continue being a leading force in the region along with the EU and keeping hope up because with a slow accession gives me concern, keeping hope up from the countries that are trying to get in, of gaining access into NATO or the EU that it, in fact, can happen. And what do we need to do to make sure that that happens?

So I will get off my bandwagon. The question, for example, I get concerned about whether or not the dates and framework is still salvageable. I get—the questions that I have, so I want to throw that out. The question that I have is that since 2013, what progress has been made since Serbia and Kosovo signed the Agreement of Principles and Governing, the normalization of relations, and do both sides remain fully committed to the process. And if not, who is not? What can we do to help so that they can be committed to the process? I want to look at it on a positive side so that we can figure out how we can work this thing to make it happen so that we can be—we still are striving, we are never going to be perfect, but continue to striving to be better and working to be better and having it more in an integrated and therefore co-dependent scenario.

Mr. Vejvoda?

Mr. VEJVODA. Thank you very much, Congressman Meeks, for those questions. First of all on Dayton, and the 20th anniversary, there is a very concrete now proposal that is a joint German-British proposal of Ministers Steinmeier and Hammond that came out in November about how to kick start, to put it very simply, Bosnia out of this stagnation, both politically and economically. They both visited the region recently. As a consequence, Bosnia, the Parliament, the new Parliament that was voted in recently and the new government signed on the dotted line that they would work within this proposal on how to find socioeconomic steps forward and also importantly, they were given the next step in EU integration which is called the Stabilization and Association Agreement that by the way Kosovo will be getting in a few months, if not weeks, if my dates are correct. That was announced by the EU Special Representation Samuel Zbogar just 2 or 3 days ago in Pristina.

So I think again the EU, with all of its troubles and slowness, is a tanker that moves ahead and the enlargement progress writ large is moving in spite of what was mentioned about the fatigue. And obviously, European countries are also in a process of what is called renationalization because everybody has economic and social problems and thus, they don't want to be seen as helping others or giving aid money when money is needed for employment.

So again, being very cautiously optimistic on Bosnia, which has been the slowest to move, identifiably, of all the countries, I think when the new government that has been established and having signed this compact with the European Union, we have to see what happens in the coming months and then come back and assess that.

On the agreement between Belgrade and Pristina and Serbia and Kosovo, I think as I said, it is a historical agreement. There is no easy way around this. Both countries know, both capitals, both prime ministers know that if they do not reach an agreement there is no help out there. There is no movement toward either the European Union or anywhere else. The EU made by its own recognition a mistake by taking in Cypress as a member state with an unresolved territorial issue. As you know, the north of the island still is under the control of Turkey. And it so happened people make mistakes and they said never again. So that means that both Belgrade and Pristina have to resolve this, sign on the dotted line in the end at the doorstep of Europe, in the door step, just after the door step and what is termed the process of normalization. This is going to last several years. Nobody is at the door step of Europe yet. I think the closest is Montenegro and after that Serbia. They both hope to finish the negotiations by 2019, 2020. And there is the ratification process.

So I think that the fact that we didn't have a government in Pristina for well close to a year hindered the advance. Again, as a citizen, I would like to see this move much more rapidly to see more movement in this direction. But again, because we are dealing with a conflict, a post-conflict situation, we have leaders who have now signed, Prime Ministers Dacic and Thachi now; today, Prime Ministers Mustafa and Vucic met in Brussels on February 9th. They made an agreement on the judiciary. They will be meeting again. The teams are meeting all the time. They have, we have not Ambassadors, but representatives on both sides sitting in Belgrade from Kosovo and vice versa. Our foreign minister was in Pristina just a month ago for a meeting of foreign meetings. There is more than meets the eye. Let me put it that way. These things do not hit the news because they are not news, if it is not something dramatic. What I am saying is we are moving slowly up the hill.

Mr. ROHRABACHER. I will give both of you a chance to give me a 2-minute closing statement.

Mr. DIOGUARDI. No questions.

Mr. ROHRABACHER. But only two. Two minutes, Joe.

Mr. DioGuardi. Let me reflect on what you said and what Mr. Vejvoda said. You know, when you talk about the young people of Kosovo and Macedonia, you are talking about 60 percent unemployment. Think about that. When you are talking about the young people in the province that is in southern Serbia, annexed illegally in 1956 from Kosovo called Presheva, Presheva Valley, three towns, Presheva, Medvedja, and Bujanovac, the unemployment is 90 percent.

Now how much longer can the Albanian people put up with this kind of isolation, no jobs, and with the highest birth rate in Europe. This is why the United States has to continue to be present aggressively in the Balkans to protect them. They have American values. They are the most multi-religious tolerant people in Europe. And I daresay, the way the Albanians in the 15th century prevented the Ottoman Turks, the barbaric Ottoman Turks, from taking over all of Europe, don't forget they took over Albania, but the Albanians wore them down for 25 years.

Remember what Mehmetd II said in 1453 when he took Constantinople and no one believed it could be done. He said, "Now we will make St. Peter's Basilica a stable for our horses." They were dead set on taking Italy and the rest of Europe. And, guess what ISIS said 3 weeks ago? "We are going to now make St. Peter's Basilica a stable for our horses." Five hundred years has passed and nothing has changed.

The only people in Europe today that are going to keep ISIS out of Europe are the Albanian people and they are doing it right now. Because they are nominally the largest Muslim population, because they were forcibly converted by the Ottoman Turks over 425 years, but they are moderate, secular, American democratic type people and we need them on our side to insure that ISIS doesn't get a foothold in Europe.

Mr. Rohrabacher. Thank you very much, Joe.

Mr. Vejvoda. Just very briefly, Chairman Rohrabacher, I am very happy to hear that you will be—you are planning to visit the region. I think that is the best way to beyond us who are testifying here today.

Mr. Rohrabacher. Mr. Meeks, we are planning to visit the region?

Mr. Meeks. Absolutely.

Mr. Rohrabacher. All right. There you go.

Mr. Vejvoda. I am glad we locked that in. So you will genuinely see for yourselves and obviously you will be meeting everyone from government and nongovernmental organizations to representatives of our minorities and our business people which is very important.

I would just like to mention that in Belgrade in September there will be a meeting of business people with all the prime ministers of the region called Southeast European Compact that was supposed to be held in March, but was delayed. It is about the credibility of the West, may I put it, of both the European Union and the United States, to see to it that these countries are finally integrated. I think there is a way to move this forward more quickly. The countries have 90 percent of the obligations to reform themselves, to put their institutions to consolidate them, make them as democratic as possible and for the citizens to be engaged and see to it that their elected officials are accountable and responsible.

Finally, I think the whole region, all of these countries individually have decided and have joined the community of values that represents the transatlantic community and I think that is the basis of the fact that this—that one can be cautiously optimistic that we are moving in the right direction.

Mr. DioGuardi. Mr. Chairman, can I just make one concluding comment? Mr. Vejvoda has to understand that Serbia works overtime to keep Kosovo out of the United Nations, although 106 countries have recognized it. And to keep them out of all European institutions. They want them completely isolated, so how can we say that we are happy with normalization and stabilization?

Mr. Rohrabacher. I promised both of you the last minute and so we are going to give you an extra 30 seconds to answer that.

Mr. Vejvoda. Actually, I would like to correct the Honorable Dio-Guardi. It is 110 countries that have recognized Kosovo, so it is going——

Mr. DioGuardi. But not Serbia or Russia or Greece.

Mr. Vejvoda. There is an example called the two Germanies that the negotiations between Belgrade and Pristina in 2007 and then under Ambassador Ischinger advocated. I think again, there is nothing simple in these processes. I think we are moving to a full normalization. I don't need to tell you that domestic politics is the key one because politicians like to be elected and they choose their moments of advance or waiting for the right moment to do the difficult decisions.

Mr. Rohrabacher. I would like to thank both of you and all of the witnesses today. I have some unconventional ideas of my own as people know, but I generally believe in self-determination and democratic government and respecting the rights of other people. And I find that there has been great double standards when people—our friends in Europe, I think World War II created a basic yearning for stability and that yearning for stability sometimes creates pressures that actually lead to problems, more problems than if people were a little bit freer and at least I would suggest less structured. And within the EU, I don't see the EU structure and NATO as being the wherewithal, but these other nations have been told it is. I mean, we will see.

I frankly see the EU as also having a lot of problems with economic elites that manipulate the rules of the game for their own benefit, sometimes, and other times for the benefit of their country. But whatever it is, we need to make sure that there are evil forces in the world beyond what we are talking about and there are evil forces. We do have an upsurge in radical Islam that could be to our civilization what the expansion of a fanatic Islam was a thousand years ago. And that would be a new threat to both western civilization.

I will have to say that if el-Sisi, for example, falls in Egypt, my guess is that Qatar, Kuwait, all of those countries will fall and you will a radical Islamic penetration into Central Asia and then with North Africa. That is what we are talking about, a great, historical change in the reality that we face today. And I think how are we going to thwart that? One way is to make sure that those Muslims who are in Europe, the Albanian people in particular, are treated fairly and their children don't find a hopelessness when they look to the future. And Joe's statistics of 60 percent unemployment in some of these areas and 90 percent in some areas, that will lead to problems, major problems and it has been 20 years. We cannot mark another 20 years and with that said I am very grateful to you, Joe, thank you, and thank to all of our witnesses. I think this hearing has been worthwhile——

Mr. VEJVODA. Yes.

Mr. ROHRABACHER [continuing]. In starting a discussion and we will finish that discussion and I will find out personally whether or not that glass in Belgrade is half full or half empty. And if it is half full, I will test it. Thank you all very much. This hearing is adjourned.

[Whereupon, at 4:41 p.m., the subcommittee was adjourned.]

APPENDIX

MATERIAL SUBMITTED FOR THE RECORD

SUBCOMMITTEE HEARING NOTICE
COMMITTEE ON FOREIGN AFFAIRS
U.S. HOUSE OF REPRESENTATIVES
WASHINGTON, D.C. 20515-6128

Subcommittee on Europe, Eurasia, and Emerging Threats
Dana Rohrabacher (R-CA), Chairman

April 22, 2015

TO: MEMBERS OF THE COMMITTEE ON FOREIGN AFFAIRS

You are respectfully requested to attend an OPEN hearing of the Committee on Foreign Affairs, to be held by the Subcommittee on Europe, Eurasia, and Emerging Threats in Room 2200 of the Rayburn House Office Building (and available on the Committee website at www.foreignaffairs.gov):

DATE: Wednesday, April 29, 2015

TIME: 2:00 p.m.

SUBJECT: Progress and Challenges in the Western Balkans

WITNESSES: Panel I
Mr. Hoyt Brian Yee
Deputy Assistant Secretary
Bureau of European and Eurasian Affairs
U.S. Department of State

Ms. Susan Fritz
Acting Assistant Administrator
Europe and Eurasia Bureau
U.S. Agency for International Development

Panel II
Mr. Ivan Vejvoda
Senior Vice President, Programs
German Marshall Fund of the United States

The Honorable Joseph J. DioGuardi
President
Albanian American Civic League
(Former Member of Congress)

By Direction of the Chairman

COMMITTEE ON FOREIGN AFFAIRS

MINUTES OF SUBCOMMITTEE ON _____ *Europe, Eurasia, and Emerging Threats* _____ HEARING

Day__ *Wednesday* __Date_____ *4/29/15* _____Room___ *Rayburn 2200* ___

Starting Time ___ *2:00 p.m.* ___ Ending Time ___ *4:41 p.m.* ___

Recesses |___| (___to ___) (___to ___) (___to ___) (___to ___) (___to ___) (___to ___)

Presiding Member(s)

Mr. Rohrabacher

Check all of the following that apply:

Open Session ☑   Electronically Recorded (taped) ☑
Executive (closed) Session ☐   Stenographic Record ☑
Televised ☑

TITLE OF HEARING:

Progress and Challenges in the Western Balkans

SUBCOMMITTEE MEMBERS PRESENT:

Mr. Meeks and Mr. Sires

NON-SUBCOMMITTEE MEMBERS PRESENT: *(Mark with an * if they are not members of full committee.)*

HEARING WITNESSES: Same as meeting notice attached? Yes ☑ No ☐
(If "no", please list below and include title, agency, department, or organization.)

STATEMENTS FOR THE RECORD: *(List any statements submitted for the record.)*

1.) Erwan Fouéré's article, "Gruevski Must Resign and Make Way for Transition Process" submitted by Chairman Rohrabacher.
2.) Shirley Cloyes Dioguardi's article ,"Confronting the Roots of Kosova's Downward Spiral" submitted by Chairman Rohrabacher.

TIME SCHEDULED TO RECONVENE _____
or
TIME ADJOURNED ___ *4:41 p.m.* ___

Subcommittee Staff Director

MATERIAL SUBMITTED FOR THE RECORD BY THE HONORABLE JOSEPH J. DIOGUARDI, PRESIDENT, ALBANIAN AMERICAN CIVIC LEAGUE (FORMER MEMBER OF CONGRESS)

Confronting the Roots of Kosova's Downward Spiral
Shirley Cloyes DioGuardi

Six years after "supervised independence" began in Kosova and fifteen years after NATO airstrikes brought an end to Serbia's genocidal war in Kosova, December 2014 marks a disappointing turning point in Kosova's recent history. The six-month stalemate in Kosova's political process, following the general elections on June 8, and ending with the breakup of the coalition that opposed the return of Hashim Thaci as prime minister and his ruling Democratic Party of Kosova (PDK), has deepened Kosova's democratic deficit. With the election in the Kosova Assembly on December 8 of Isa Mustafa as Prime Minister, Hashim Thaci as Deputy Prime Minister and Foreign Minister, and Kadri Veseli, the former head of Kosova's shadowy secret service, SHIK, as Speaker of the Parliament, along with the appointment of an excessive number of ministers and deputy ministers, the political elite that has prevented Kosova from flourishing and prospering for the past decade has returned to power.

While Belgrade has taken every measure possible since war's end to maintain its dominance over Prishtina and to destabilize Kosova and the region, and while the West has yet to grant Kosova full sovereignty and admission to international institutions, the majority of Kosova's political elite bear responsibility for the nation's political and economic deterioration because they have failed to engage seriously in state building. Instead of upholding the rule of law, they have lined their pockets by seeking kickbacks and appointing unqualified family members to important positions. Instead of fostering economic development, their privatization activities have led to questionable projects that have enriched them and their foreign partners. As a result, unemployment in Kosova is now at least 40 percent (it is over 60 percent in the 18 to 30 age group) and Kosovar youth have been leaving the country in droves, more often than not illegally.

Contrary to their statements that they played no role in ending the post-election political deadlock, both the European Union and the United States exerted significant pressure on LDK, which won 30 seats in Kosova's general elections, to abandon the larger coalition and to form a coalition with PDK, which won 37 seats in the 120-member Assembly. The West preferred the political status quo in order to advance their policy of appeasing Serbia, which they wrongly view as the future economic and political engine in Southeast Europe.

The European Union has failed Kosova's people by giving lip service to ending corruption and organized crime in Kosova and strengthening the rule of law, while simultaneously siding with the corrupt members of Kosova's political elites. The EU has become part of the problem with the recent revelation by a British whistle blower that judges and prosecutors representing the European Union Rule of Law Mission (EULEX) have shielded powerful politicians by covering up evidence of their corruption. The EU has also turned Kosova into the last European "ghetto" by rewarding Serbia and not granting Kosova visa liberalization—something that the Kosova Assembly should call for immediately.

Visa liberalization is essential not only for economic development, but also because Kosova's isolation has given rise to the unprecedented and dangerous incursion of radical Islam. While

Kosovars are prevented from traveling to Western Europe and the United States, they are free to travel east to Turkey and beyond. Islamic fundamentalists from the Arab world have been financing political movements, building mosques where none ever existed before in Kosova, and giving money to poverty-stricken women in exchange for their wearing the veil and sending their sons to religious schools. For the first time since 1912 (when the 425-year occupation of Albanian lands by the Ottoman Turkish Empire was overthrown), Islamic fundamentalists, widely rejected by Albanians all over the Balkans, have managed to infiltrate a population of secular Muslims, who have lived side by side their Roman Catholic, Eastern Orthodox Christian, and Jewish neighbors in harmony for centuries. Radical Islam is counter to the Albanian model of Islam, the core of which is interfaith tolerance, respect, and understanding.

The U.S. government has also failed Kosova's people by joining the European Union in propping up Kosova's corrupt political elites. In the process, America has abused its clout among Albanians, the most pro-American, pro-democratic ethnic group in Southeast Europe. By handing the reins of power after the war almost exclusively to those political leaders who would comply with Western mandates, the West failed to harness the education and expertise of many Kosovar professionals. By continually taking a backseat to Europe, US Administrations have enabled Belgrade to move into the vacuum created by the lack of unity and resolve of the EU's twenty-eight member nations, five of which refuse to recognize Kosova as an independent state.

At the same time, too many Kosovars think of themselves as an oppressed minority, subject to the whims of Serbia, Russia, and the European Union conspiring against the newest country in the world. The reality is that Albanians are the overwhelming majority of a new state and instead of lamenting genuine and imagined threats to Kosova's existence, elected officials need to get down to the business of governing, of policing, of providing energy, water, adequate education, and healthcare to all of its citizens, and of introducing anti-corruption measures in every public body, both local and national.

The Kosova government has the power to alter the future of the Prishtina-Belgrade talks by taking control of relations with Serbs in northern Kosova. It also has the power to resist the creation of a special war crimes tribunal for Kosova, when so very few Serbian paramilitary and military troops have been brought to justice for the ten-year occupation of Kosova, the expulsion of a million Kosovars, and the murder and rape of thousands with seeming impunity from 1998 to 1999. The Kosova government could concentrate on bringing this injustice into the international spotlight. It is simply a matter of political will.

Kosova can succeed, but it cannot do so unless Kosovars rise up in the face of adversity and become the masters of their own destiny. It is time for Kosovars, especially the youth, to seize the moment and initiate nonviolent action to bring international attention to Kosova's downward spiral. It is also time for capable men and women in the Albanian diaspora—too many of whom have turned their backs on Kosova since independence was declared in 2008—to help Kosova move out of the desperate social and economic situation that the country finds itself in. Otherwise, Kosova will continue its drift into a state of economic and political limbo, and it will be at the constant mercy of external powers.

Ossining, New York
December 29, 2014

Shirley Cloyes DioGuardi, a foreign policy analyst specializing in the Balkan conflict, is Balkan Affairs Adviser to the Albanian American Civic League.

MATERIAL SUBMITTED FOR THE RECORD BY THE HONORABLE JOSEPH J. DIOGUARDI, PRESIDENT, ALBANIAN AMERICAN CIVIC LEAGUE (FORMER MEMBER OF CONGRESS)

Gruevski Must Resign and Make Way For Transition Process

It is time for the Macedonian Prime Minister to go - any other solution would be like rearranging the deck chairs on a sinking ship.

By Erwan Fouéré

As the revelations from the wiretapping scandal reverberate across Macedonia and beyond, the extent of the alleged corruption and intimidation perpetrated by the Prime Minister, Nikola Gruevski and his ruling party VMRO-DPMNE has been brought out into the open.

Shocking details of how laws and democratic standards have been violated or simply ignored by government ministers and senior officials highlight the impunity and cavalier behaviour of a regime with none of the system of accountability one would expect in a normal democratic society.

Erwan Fouéré

Claims by the Prime Minister that the wiretapping is the work of foreign intelligence services fool nobody, while his accusation that opposition leader Zoran Zaev plotted a coup reflects the government's determination to find any excuse to silence its political opponents.

Judging from the allegations of opposition leader, that this vast wiretapping operation has been going on for several years, one can only surmise with some trepidation what has yet to be revealed, particularly in relation to inter-ethnic issues.

The government led by Nikola Gruevski has been marked by repeated tensions between the ethnic Albanian and majority Macedonian communities, often provoked by the ruling party's lack of sensitivity to the multi-ethnic character of the country.

Instead of promoting a policy of unity, the ruling party, through its aggressive pursuit of the controversial Skopje 2014 project, for example, has jeopardized the delicate balance that has kept the country together since the Ohrid Framework Agreement was signed in 2001.

Nor has the content of the wiretapping of foreign diplomatic missions yet been revealed. The mere fact that such wiretapping allegedly took place will have serious international implications, not least because of the government's international obligations under the Vienna Convention.

This is clearly a regime living on borrowed time. Having lost whatever credibility and legitimacy it had to remain the government, the Prime Minister should put the interests of the country at heart and tender his resignation together with the entire cabinet.

Suggestions that some of his ministers most directly implicated should resign, such as the Interior and Transport Ministers, while the Prime Minister himself remains in office, would be like rearranging the deck chairs on a sinking ship.

According to recent statements made by the Commissioner Johannes Hahn, the EU - whose leaders have been very slow in grasping the extent of the unfolding crisis - seems to be opting for a mediation effort to be undertaken by a delegation from the European Parliament.

This raises many questions, not least one of the ethics in trying to mediate with a ruling party that has lost whatever moral authority it had and, judging from the content of the released tapes, behaves in an autocratic manner, ignoring the rule of law and institutional process.

It is also doubtful that such a mediation effort has much chance of success, if past experience is anything to go by. The last mediation effort that involved the European Parliament was launched in March 2013 in an attempt to overcome the crisis caused by the physical expulsion of all the opposition MPs and journalists from the Parliament in December 2012. It was not crowned in glory, with the ruling party disowning part of the compromise agreement reached several months later as "toilet paper".

The only way out of this crisis is for the current government to resign and make way for the start of a transitional process.

This transitional process would have three broad strands:

- to prepare the country for a proper electoral process free from the irregularities and intimidation which have marred so many past elections, as amply documented by the official OSCE/ODIHR election observation reports. Sufficient time should be set aside for this purpose to ensure that all elements of the electoral process, including proper control over use of state funds, financing of political parties and guarantee of independent media are effectively addressed; the Independent Electoral Commission should be strengthened with support from international experts.

- an independent commission of inquiry should be established with the direct involvement of internationally respected personalities. The commission's task would be to investigate all aspects of the wiretapping allegations and it should have the power to call witnesses. This would ensure an objective assessment, free from political interference. Leaving this work to the current public prosecutor and judicial system would have no credibility in view of the direct interference by the ruling party in the judicial process over the past years, a point underlined in the European Commission Progress Reports. The Commission should have its work completed and a report made public before the holding of elections.

- a critical role should be played by civil society organisations, the academic community and the media in promoting open debates and dialogue across the country, free from the threats of intimidation that have been the hallmark of the current political environment. This would help to restore the social fabric of a society deeply traumatized by years of divisive politics where people were categorized as either patriots or traitors and enemies of the state. It would also contribute towards reducing the intolerance and deep mistrust between the ethnic communities, and would allow moderate voices including new political forces to emerge.

This is a critical time for Macedonia. Either it continues to sink further into the abyss under the current regime, or it takes a courageous step in breaking with the current system and works towards restoring basic democratic values and standards. It is for the Macedonian people to decide, in an environment free from the deceit, dishonesty, intimidation and fear that have marked the past years. The international community, in particular the EU and the OSCE, must be there to offer help and guidance.

Erwan Fouéré is Associate Senior Research Fellow at the Centre for European Policy Studies, and was the EU Special Representative in Macedonia from 2005 to 2011.